PAUL E. SPECTOR

SAS®

PROGRAMMING

for

RESEARCHERS

and

SOCIAL
SCIENTISTS

SECOND EDITION

Sage Publications
International Educational and Professional Publisher
Thousand Oaks ▪ London ▪ New Delhi

The sample program logs and output in this book were generated using SAS/STAT software, version 8.01 of the SAS System for Windows. Copyright © 2000 SAS Institute Inc. SAS and all other SAS Institute Inc. product or service names are registered trademarks or trademarks of SAS Institute Inc., Cary, NC, USA.

For information:

Sage Publications, Inc.
2455 Teller Road
Thousand Oaks, California 91320
E-mail: order@sagepub.com

Sage Publications Ltd.
6 Bonhill Street
London EC2A 4PU
United Kingdom

Sage Publications India Pvt. Ltd.
M-32 Market
Greater Kailash I
New Delhi 110 048 India

Printed in the United States of America

Library of Congress Cataloging-in-Publication Data

Spector, Paul E.
  SAS® programming for researchers and social scientists / by Paul E. Spector.— 2nd ed.
    p. cm.
  Includes bibliographical references and index.
  ISBN 0-7619-2267-9 (cloth: alk. paper)
  ISBN 0-7619-2268-7 (pbk.: alk. paper)
  1. SAS (Computer file) 2. Social sciences—Statistics—Data processing. I. Title.
QA276.4 .S645 2001
519.5'0285'53—dc21   00-012751

03 04 05 06 10 9 8 7 6 5 4 3

Acquiring Editor:	C. Deborah Laughton
Editorial Assistant:	Eileen Carr
Production Editor:	Nevair Kabakian
Editorial Assistant:	Kathryn Journey
Typesetter/Designer:	Denyse Dunn
Cover Designer:	Michelle Lee

SAS®
PROGRAMMING
for
RESEARCHERS
and
SOCIAL
SCIENTISTS

SECOND EDITION

Contents

Preface   **xi**
What's New in the Second Edition   xiv
Acknowledgments   xv

1. Introduction to the SAS® System   **1**
What Makes the SAS System a Computer Language?   2
Example of a SAS Program   3
Different Releases and Versions of the SAS System   5
A SAS Programming Session With the Windows Version   6
   Overview of the SAS System Interface, Release 6.11   7
   Overview of the SAS System Interface, Release 8.01   9
   Running Program 1.1 With the Windows Version   12
How to Approach Programming a Problem   15
Debugging a Program   17
   Types of Errors   18
   Finding Errors   19
SAS Statements   21
Additional Help   22
Using This Book   24
Debugging Exercises   25

2. Inputting and Outputting Data   **27**
Defining a Data Step   28
Location of the Data Set to Input   31
   Inside the Program   32
   External File   32
   SAS Data Library   33
Inputting Data Lines   34

	Specifying Column Locations	35
	W.d Formats	35
	Character Values	38
	List Input	38
	Holding the Input Line	40
	Controlling Output to the SAS Data Set	41
	Specifying the Location for Outputting	42
	Formatting the Output	43
	PROC PRINT	44
	Example of Inputting and Outputting	45
	Writing Reports With PUT Statements	48
	Using PROC PRINT and PUT for Debugging	52
	Common Errors	53
	Debugging Exercises	53
3.	**Programming Algebraic and Mathematical Operations**	**55**
	Arithmetic Operators	56
	SAS Functions	59
	ABS	59
	Descriptive Statistics Functions	61
	Log and Exponential Functions	63
	MOD	63
	Factorials, Combinations, and Permutations (Release 8)	63
	Probability Distributions	64
	Random Number Generators	64
	Rounding Functions	65
	SQRT	66
	Trigonomic Functions	66
	Deleting Variables From a SAS Data Set	67
	Examples Using Functions	68
	Common Errors	72
	Debugging Exercises	73
4.	**Logical Statements**	**75**
	Program to Screen for Data Errors	79
	The ELSE Statement	81
	Selecting and Deleting Cases From a SAS Data Set	82
	Detecting the End of a File	83
	Executing Several Statements After an IF . . . THEN	84
	Overriding Case-by-Case Resetting of Variable Values	84
	Accumulators and Counters	86

	Computing an Independent Group *t* Test	87
	Common Errors	91
	Debugging Exercises	92
5.	**Branching With GOTO and LINK**	**95**
	GOTO Statement	96
	LINK Statement	97
	RETURN Statement	97
	STOP Statement	98
	OUTPUT Statement Revisited	98
	Flags	99
	A More Complex Example of Statement Control	101
	Program Flow	105
	Common Errors	107
	Debugging Exercises	109
6.	**Do Loops**	**111**
	DO Index=	112
	DO UNTIL	113
	DO WHILE	115
	Coin Flip Simulation With a Do Loop	117
	Nested Loops	118
	Simulation of the Violation of *t-Test Assumptions*	121
	Common Errors	126
	Debugging Exercises	128
7.	**Arrays**	**129**
	ARRAY Statement	130
	One-Dimensional Arrays	131
	Scoring Psychological Tests With Arrays	132
	Multidimensional Arrays	137
	Handling Two-Dimensional Data Using Multidimensional Arrays	140
	Programming Matrix Algebra Operations	142
	Matrix Transpose	144
	Matrix Multiplication	144
	The SSCP Matrix Program	145
	Common Errors	148
	Debugging Exercises	149
8.	**Manipulating Files**	**151**
	Inputting Multiple Files	151
	Concatenation	152
	Merging	153

Sorting With PROC SORT 156
Inputting From and Outputting to SAS Data Library Files 157
Outputting Multiple Data Sets 159
   Outputting to SAS Data Sets 160
   Outputting to Non-SAS Files 161
Combining Data From Several Files 162
Creating Multiple Files 165
   Deleting Cases With Missing Values 169
Common Errors 171
Debugging Exercises 172

9. Using SAS® PROCs **175**
Turnover Among University Clerical Workers 176
Correlations With PROC CORR 177
Frequency Tables With PROC FREQ 179
Descriptive Statistics With PROC MEANS 188
Scatterplots With PROC PLOT 188
t Tests With PROC TTEST 190
Complex Statistics 191
   Multiple Regression 193
   One-Way ANOVA 195
   Factorial ANOVA 196
   Factor Analysis 198
Common Errors 201
Resources for Information About Using PROCs 201

10. Final Advice on Becoming a SAS® Programmer **205**
Debugging and Testing a Program Revisited 206
Alternate Approaches 206
Advance Planning 208
How to Become a Good Programmer 209

Appendix A: Definitions of Useful Programming Terms   211

Appendix B: Summary of SAS Language Statements   213

Appendix C: Summary of Popular SAS PROCs   215

Appendix D: Sources of Information About Using
SAS PROCs for Statistical Analysis   219

Appendix E: Corrections to the Debugging Exercises   221

References   225

Index   227

About the Author   231

Preface

The SAS® System is a powerful tool for the manipulation and analysis of data. It is the most widely used computer statistics package available today. It is also a full-featured, high-level computer language designed specifically for the manipulation of statistical data. Whereas a number of books are available for the statistics aspect of the SAS System, only a few sources can be found that offer instruction about how to use the language features. The documentation made available by the SAS Institute Inc. provides a thorough reference to the SAS language, but it is not easy to understand by researchers and social scientists who are new to programming. The idea to write the current book came from seeing how psychology doctoral students in methodology classes struggled to learn the SAS language from the manuals alone.

The purpose of the present book is to provide instruction about how to write computer programs with the SAS language. Its intended audience includes social scientists, researchers, and others who wish to learn how to write programs with the SAS language. Although the examples come mainly from the social sciences, they should be accessible to those in other fields such as business, engineering, medicine, or the natural sciences. The book assumes that the reader has little or no knowledge of programming or the SAS language, although even experienced SAS users might find much of the material useful. Basic programming concepts, such as arrays, branching, counters, loops, inputting, and outputting are introduced in a logical sequence. Examples and sample programs are used to introduce various programming concepts in the context of common research problems. Debugging exercises in the first eight chapters help develop skills in finding programming errors. Early chapters illustrate very simple tasks, such as computing means and using functions to compute exact probabilities of statistical tests. Later chapters progress to writing programs to conduct computer simulations of statistics (with random number generators), screen data sets for errors, score psychological tests, and perform matrix operations.

The present book adopts a problem-solving approach that focuses on common programming tasks frequently encountered in conducting data analysis. Each chapter introduces several programming features of the SAS language. Specific data analysis problems are then presented with SAS programs that use the features introduced in the chapter. For each sample program, the underlying logical approach and structure are discussed. Then the book explains the program statement by statement. The reader is encouraged to enter and run each example, then experiment with modifications. Several of the examples can be adapted to real problems that the reader may have. Programs are provided for the following tasks:

1. Scan a data set for out of range variable values or impossible combinations of variable values.

2. Modify data in a file.

3. Score psychological tests.

4. Combine multiple data files.

5. Simulate the distribution of coin flips.

6. Simulate the Type 1 error rate of the *t* test when assumptions are violated.

In addition to covering program features of the SAS language, the current book also provides advice about how to learn the SAS language and how to use it efficiently. The first and last chapters focus specifically on how to approach a particular programming problem, the need for thorough planning of a program, the necessity for testing, and debugging. The book also offers encouragement about maintaining motivation when encountering the constant string of errors that are part of the programming process. Each chapter discusses common errors found with the language features introduced and offers advice about avoiding them. The book teaches principles of structured programming, advising the novice (as well as the experienced programmer) to write programs that are orderly and to avoid excessive and disorganized branching. The use of the GOTO statement is discouraged in favor of using various Do loops and

LINK statements. The idea of spaghetti code and how to avoid it is discussed. Finally, tips about helpful features and practices to use and pitfalls to avoid are offered throughout the book.

The book begins with an introduction to computer programming with the SAS language. It mentions that there are many different versions of the SAS system for different kinds of computers and different operating systems. Detailed instructions are given for using the Windows® version of the SAS System, both Release 6.11 and the newest Release 8.01, which was introduced in 2000. A general three-step approach to programming is provided that includes prior planning, writing the program, and debugging. Planning tools such as pseudocode and flowcharting are covered.

Chapters 2-8 cover various features of the SAS language introduced in a logical sequence. Chapter 2 discusses the inputting and outputting of data. The reader is shown how to use output features of the SAS language to write reports.

Chapter 3 covers the programming of algebraic and mathematical operations with expressions and functions. A subset of SAS functions is covered, including descriptive statistics functions, probability distribution functions, and random number generators.

Chapter 4 discusses logical statements using the IF . . . THEN. Program features for detecting the end of an input file are covered. Procedures for programming counters and accumulators are included in this chapter.

Chapter 5 is devoted to branching with the GOTO and LINK statements. The idea of assuming control over automatic features is covered, such as outputting cases to the SAS data set (with OUTPUT) and stopping execution (with STOP). Advice about avoiding spaghetti code and minimizing the use of the GOTO statement is given here.

Chapter 6 covers how to program Do loops with the SAS language. DO Index=, DO UNTIL, and DO WHILE are included. The use of nested loops is illustrated with a program that simulates the Type 1 error rate for a *t* test with the assumption of variance homogeneity violated in the presence of unequal sample sizes.

Chapter 7 focuses on arrays. Both one-dimensional and multidimensional arrays are covered. Matrix algebra operations are used to illustrate the use of arrays.

Chapter 8 covers the manipulation of multiple data files. The idea of merging and concatenating files with the SAS language is included, as well as reading from and writing to SAS data libraries. Procedures for producing multiple files from single files are also covered.

Chapter 9 is an introduction to SAS PROCs, which are the built-in statistics programs in the SAS system. Five PROCs to compute simple statistics are covered. They are PROC CORR to compute correlations, PROC FREQ to create frequency tables, PROC MEANS to calculate descriptive statistics, PROC PLOT to create scatterplots, and PROC TTEST to compute *t* tests. Four PROCs to compute complex statistics are also covered. They are PROC REG to conduct multiple regression, PROC ANOVA to conduct simple ANOVA, PROC GLM for factorial ANOVA with unequal sample sizes in cells, and PROC FACTOR for factor analysis. Examples of the use of these PROCs are provided, using data from an actual study of employee turnover.

Chapter 10 gives additional advice about learning how to program and enhancing programming skills. It discusses strategies for debugging and testing a program, alternate approaches to programming a problem, and the need for advanced planning. It also offers encouragement to maintain effort while developing programming skills.

WHAT'S NEW IN THE SECOND EDITION

The second edition of this book incorporates changes in both computing and the SAS System that have occurred since the early 1990s. When I wrote the first edition, researchers were using many different versions of SAS on PCs, mainframes, and UNIX workstations. Today most researchers as well as students use the Windows 95/98/2000 version of SAS for the PC. In this edition of the book, detailed instructions for using the SAS Windows interface for both Release 6.11 and Release 8.01 are included. More has been added on debugging, and there are sections in Chapters 1-9 concerning common errors. Debugging exercises (sample programs with errors) are now provided for Chapters 1-8. Five appendices have been added. Two summarize the terms and commands used throughout the book, two provide information about SAS statistical procedures or PROCs, and the last explains the errors in each of the debugging exercises.

New for the second edition is availability of supplemental Web materials. A section of my Web site (http://chuma.cas.usf.edu/~Spector) provides extra SAS help. I teach an online SAS course, and that course can be found here. Students are welcome to take all or part of the course in self-study.

Instructors are welcome to make use of this material, provided that they give appropriate credit and the use is for a noncommercial educational purpose. The site also contains some practice data sets and a few useful links, such as to the SAS Institute.

ACKNOWLEDGMENTS

I would like to thank several people whose efforts assisted me in writing this book. I am indebted to the Sage reviewers, J. Philip Craiger, who reviewed both editions, and Robert Pavur and James P. Whittenburg, who had good advice that greatly improved the book. I appreciate the efforts of my Sage editor, C. Deborah Laughton, who always had good ideas and helped me plan the approaches for both editions. I thank Kimberly Hoffman, who tested all the programs in the book. Finally, I would like to thank Gail and Steven Spector for their encouragement and patience as I wrote and then revised this book.

Chapter 1

Introduction to the SAS® System

The SAS System is arguably the most popular computer software for conducting statistical data analysis. Its popularity is due to its tremendous breadth and flexibility, in terms of both its programmability and its built-in statistical procedures. It is widely known that the SAS System contains an extensive library of statistical procedures or PROCs that can be used to conduct analyses from simple descriptive statistics up to the most complex multivariate, such as factor analysis. What is less known is that the SAS System contains a full-featured high-level computer program language. Virtually any statistical procedure, whether it is available in a PROC or not, can be programmed in the SAS language. This dual nature of the SAS System, being both a canned statistics program and a programming language, makes it an extremely powerful tool for data analysis.

This book will focus mainly on the language aspects of the SAS System. It is intended to be an introduction to computer programming with the SAS language. It assumes that you have little or no knowledge of programming, and that you may or may not be familiar with statistical data analysis with the SAS System. The book will introduce you to programming features, such as loops, arrays, and counters (Appendix A contains definitions of several commonly used programming terms). It will also show you how to implement these features with the SAS language. If you don't know what these features are, you will by the time you get to the end of this book. In addition, several basic PROCs will be covered in Chapter 9. This chapter will illustrate how PROCs can be used to simplify the programming work necessary to conduct data analyses, as well as how the language features can be used in combination with PROCs.

WHAT MAKES THE SAS SYSTEM A COMPUTER LANGUAGE?

A computer language, like a human language, provides a means for you to communicate and interact with your computer. It allows you to specify a series of commands or operations that the computer will carry out to achieve a purpose. For example, with the SAS System you can write a program to compute the mean of a series of numbers that you put in a computer document or data file. The program would tell the computer the name of the file, how to read the numbers from the file, how to do the computation, and how to display the results. Whereas many pieces of computer software, ranging from word processors to games, allow you to communicate and give commands to carry out a purpose (such as writing a letter), a computer language allows you to build your own software to accomplish a variety of tasks and is far more flexible.

Many different computer languages have been developed. For a PC or Apple Macintosh, a variety of general purpose languages are available, such as Basic, C, Fortran, and Visual Basic. All of these can be used to conduct statistical data analysis; however, they are general purpose programs that are not designed specifically for statistics. This means that they are more difficult to use and tend to run analyses more slowly. There also exist a variety of programs designed to do data and statistical analysis, such as EXCEL and SPSS. They can do many of the same things but do not provide the extensive programming capabilities of the SAS System. The SAS System is a language that was designed from the ground up to do statistical data analysis. Because it is specialized, it is designed in a way that makes programming data analysis easy and efficient. For many tasks that researchers do, the SAS language is the language of choice.

A computer program is a series of written step-by-step instructions or commands that tell the computer exactly what to do. The commands must be in the correct order and in a form that the SAS System can understand. The program you write must be perfect because the SAS System will do exactly what you tell it to do, in precisely the order you tell it, regardless of what you actually want it to do. Although the program will give you error messages when it doesn't understand a command (when the format of the command is not allowable), it blindly carries out your every instruction and is unaware of what you really want it to do.

A program is a sequential series of commands. You write your program, and then when you want it to run you tell the computer to **execute** it. Execution begins with the first command statement and then proceeds in order, statement by statement. Therefore, you must be precise, and you must tell the computer everything that must be done in the correct order. Any missing detail or command out of order can result in a wrong computation. This is both the challenge and frustration of programming. The work is meticulous and precise. On the other hand, programming can be fun, as it is very much like solving a puzzle. You begin with certain elements and must achieve a correct solution.

EXAMPLE OF A SAS PROGRAM

The three major components of most programs are data input, manipulation, and output. Although data can be generated within the program, which is done with computer simulations, most of the time data are placed into a data file and inputted into the program. These data are then manipulated to accomplish the tasks for which the program was written. This might involve transforming or combining variables or conducting statistical or other types of analyses. Finally, for the program to be of value, its results must somehow be outputted—to either a file, the screen, or paper. If you were to write a program to conduct a statistical analysis, for example, you would output a report with the results.

Program 1.1 is a simple example that illustrates the three major components. Its purpose is to calculate the mean of five numbers. The numbers are inputted, the mean is calculated, and the results are outputted. Output with the Windows version that most people use is to the output window of the SAS System interface, but with other versions output might be to a file that can be viewed on a computer monitor or to a printer. Line numbers have been added to the example programs in this book to make it easier to refer to them. Line numbering should NOT be done in a SAS program, as it will cause errors. Also note that some of the statements have been indented. This is done to make the program more readable. With long and complex programs, indenting can make it easier to trace through a program. Indenting has no effect on the execution of a program.

The first line of the program, DATA TEST, tells the SAS System that you wish to begin a data step, and that the data step will create a SAS data set called TEST. The SAS data set can have any name from 1 to 32 characters (8 for Release 6 family and earlier) long. It is helpful to give a name to a SAS data set that refers to its purpose.

Line 2 of the program says that you will have five variables, and it defines their names to be A, B, C, D, and E. Again, it is helpful to use variable names that reflect the nature of the data. For every case that might be entered, the variables must be in the same order.

Line 3 calculates the sum of the five variables. Line 4 divides the total by 5 to calculate the mean.

The fifth line tells the computer that you wish to output the results to the print location. In the old mainframe days, this meant going straight to the printer. With the newer PC versions, this will display the output on the screen. The sixth line tells the computer how you wish to print the results. This statement will produce the output:

```
MEAN = 3
```

The seventh line says that what follows will be data to be inputted according to the format specified in line 2. The eighth line contains the data for the example. Line 9, containing only a semicolon, indicates that there are no more data.

Line 10 contains a RUN statement, which instructs the SAS System to execute the preceding statements. On some systems the RUN statement is necessary to make your program execute. All examples in this book will include this statement.

Of course you wouldn't go to the bother of writing a SAS program like this one to compute the mean of five numbers. It would take longer to write the program than it would to compute the answer by hand. Furthermore, SAS has PROCs and built-in functions to compute simple statistics like means. It is often necessary to write programs to prepare data for analysis with PROCs or to do analyses not available in PROCs.

Program 1.1

Example of a SAS® Program

```
 1 DATA TEST;
 2 INPUT A B C D E;
 3 TOTAL = A + B + C + D + E;
 4 MEAN = TOTAL/5;
 5 FILE PRINT;
 6 PUT 'MEAN = ' MEAN;
 7 DATALINES;
 8 1 2 3 4 5
 9 ;
10 RUN;
```

DIFFERENT RELEASES AND VERSIONS OF THE SAS SYSTEM

Versions of the SAS System have been adapted to many different types of computers including mainframes, UNIX workstations, and personal computers. Most students and individual researchers today use the SAS System for the personal computer (PC) running Windows 95/98/2000 (hereafter referred to as Windows). An advantage of this version is that it provides a nice graphical Windows interface with which you can write and enter your program and retrieve the output. Versions for other types of computers are different, and not all have a graphical interface. Although the interface of the SAS System differs across versions, there are only minor differences in the programming language component that is the main topic for this book. The major difference is in how you specify the names of files for inputting and outputting data. This book will concentrate on the Windows version of the interface and will explain how it can be used.

In addition to the various versions of SAS for different computer systems, there have been different generations of the software, called releases. The first edition of this book was designed for the 6.11 release of the SAS System. Keep in mind that there were several releases in the 6.x family that had fairly minor differences. In the spring of 2000, the SAS Institute produced a major upgrade in Release 8.0, and as of this writing Release 8.01 is available. The Release 8.x family provides many significant improvements to the Windows interface for the SAS software, making it much easier to use. It also expanded some of the programming features, although most are not covered in this basic book. Throughout the book I will use Release 6 and 8 to refer to the entire family or series of releases.

Because it will take several years until Release 8 takes over completely from the various 6 releases, this book will provide instruction for both. For the most part, programs written for one release will run on the other, and where there are differences, they will be noted. Generally, programs written for newer releases will run without modification on older, but the opposite is not always true, as over time new features and enhancements have been added. All the example programs in this book will run on both releases. Where differences exist, they will be noted.

If you are using one of the Release 6s, there are enough enhancements to make it worth upgrading to the newest Release 8.01 (or later versions as they become available), provided you have the hardware to handle it. A basic installation of just the base software and statistics takes about 250 megs of hard drive space, which is about double that taken by Release 6.11. If you are a serious user of SAS, it might be worth upgrading your computer to be able to use Release 8.01. The improvements to the Program Editor alone make it worthwhile.

A SAS PROGRAMMING SESSION WITH THE WINDOWS VERSION

Assuming that the SAS System has been loaded on your computer, a session begins by starting the SAS software so that it will appear on the screen. Depending on how the SAS system has been placed on the computer, you might start the SAS System by clicking on an icon on the desktop or by clicking on the Start button and going to Programs to find the SAS System. The different releases and subreleases have somewhat different looks. Although the major components of the design have remained more or less the same, there have been significant improvements from release to release. Below we will describe the SAS System Interface for Release 6.11 and Release 8.01. Other releases are somewhat different.

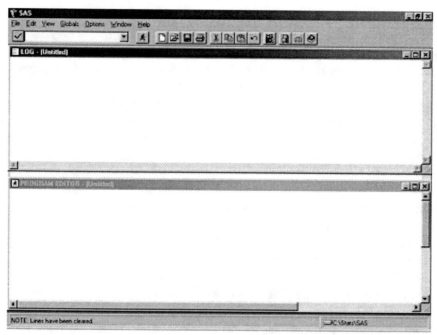

Figure 1.1. Illustration of the Windows 95/98/2000 SAS System Interface for SAS Release 6.11

Overview of the SAS System Interface, Release 6.11

When you first start the SAS System, it will fill your screen and probably look like Figure 1.1. As you can see in the figure, this version of SAS looks very much like a typical Windows program. At the top are pulldown menus and buttons. In the middle there's space for you to write your program and see results.

There are three separate windows that you will use in writing and running your program. The first is the **program editor**, which is at the bottom of the figure, below where it says "PROGRAM EDITOR—(Untitled)." This is a space where you can write your program commands to be executed later. It works like a simple text editor or word processor. You can enter your commands, edit them, save the program, and load it. Once you have the program written, you can run or **execute** it (we will see how to do this later). The second window is the **log**, which contains error messages and other important information to help you determine if the program worked correctly. It is above the program editor in the figure, below where it says "LOG—(Untitled)." The third window, which isn't shown in the figure, is the **output**, where the results of your program are displayed. It is possible to configure your SAS System to display all three windows at once. It is also possible to expand one of the windows to take up the entire workspace below the toolbar (the row of icons above the log window). An easy way to do this is to click on the square in the upper right-hand corner of the log, output, or program editor window. An easy way to move from one window to the other is with the F keys in the top row of your keyboard. Table 1.1 shows the most commonly used F keys.

The pulldown menus at the top of Figure 1.1 contain the commands you will need to run the SAS software interface. Although it is beyond our scope to cover them in detail, I will point out the most important. As is typical of most Windows software, under **File** you will find commands to open files, save files, and print. There is one caution. Contrary to standard Windows practice, when opening and saving files, the default with the SAS System interface is to save to the most recently saved file rather than the most recently opened file. With most other software, if you open a file (let's call it one.sas), and then save it, and then you open a second file (let's call it two.sas), and then save it, the default name will be two.sas. With SAS, the default name will be one.sas because that is the most recent file saved. Where this causes a problem is that it is very easy to save one file, then open another and save it over the first one. To avoid this, always be extremely careful when saving a file that the name you are about to save to is really the one you intend. With most Windows software, the default name is the one for the file you just opened, so it's easy to get in the habit of quickly clicking on **Save** as, then on *Save* without paying close attention to the file name.

The next pulldown is **Edit**, which contains the commands to cut and paste part of your program in the Program Editor window. It also allows you to do find, and find and replace, functions. Under **Globals**, then **Options**, then Global Options, you can set various options for your programming session, including how many characters are printed in a line in the Output window, or how many times an error message will be repeated in the log. **Options** allows you to set options for your SAS System interface, such as the size and type of font to be displayed, and what to put in the menu bar.

Table 1.1

Most Common F Key Functions in the SAS System

F Key	Function
F1	Bring up the help window
F4	Recall the program after it executes
F5	Go to the Program Editor
F6	Go to the Log
F7	Go to the Output
F8	Execute the program
F9	Show the F keys
F11	Go to the command bar to enter a command

On the left-hand side of the menu bar is a white space, or **command bar**, where you can write commands (look to the right of the check mark in the upper left corner of Figure 1.1). You can click on the white space with your mouse or press the F11 key to put a cursor in the command bar so you can type a command. The command will work for whichever of the three windows you have active. From here you can enlarge the window by typing "zoom," or erase the window by typing "clear." The commands you use in your SAS session will be saved, and you can use them by clicking on the little down arrowhead (upside-down triangle) just to the right of the command bar. To the right of the command bar are icons that you can use to do some of the most common tasks, such as open a file, print, run the program, and help.

Overview of the SAS System Interface, Release 8.01

When you first start the SAS System, it will fill your screen and probably look like Figure 1.2. As you can see in the figure, this version of SAS looks very much like a typical Windows program. At the top are pulldown menus and buttons. In the middle there's space for you to write your program and see results. To the left is the Explorer, which gives you quick access to your SAS libraries and other files, as well as files containing results of your programs. There are additional buttons on the bottom to allow you to switch easily from screen to screen. All of this can be customized to your own preferences.

There are three separate windows that you will use in writing and running your program. The first is the editor, which is at the bottom of the figure, below where it says "Editor—Untitled1." This is a space where you can write your program commands to be executed later. It works like a simple text editor or word processor. You can enter your commands, edit them, save the program, and load it. There are two types of editors—the regular editor, which works very much like the 6.11 variety, and the advanced editor, which does some useful extra functions that will be discussed in the following paragraph. Once you have the program written you can run or execute it (we will see how to do this later). The second window is the log, which contains error messages and other important information to help you determine if the program worked correctly. It is above the editor in the figure, below where it says "LOG—(Untitled)." The third window, which isn't shown in the figure, is the output, where the results of your program are displayed. It is possible to configure your SAS System to display all three windows at once. It is also possible to expand one of the windows to take up the entire workspace below the toolbar (the row of icons above the log window). An easy way to do this is to click on the square in the upper right-hand corner of the Log, Output, or Editor window. The buttons that are below the editor window can be used to move from one window to the other. There is a button for the Output, Log, and Editor windows. You can also use the function or F keys in the top row of your keyboard. Table 1.1 shows the most commonly used F keys. It is possible to change the function of each key from the screen that is displayed when you press the F9 key.

With SAS 8.01, there are two different editors. The Program Editor works very much like the one in Release 6.11. It allows you to enter your program statements and then execute them. After execution you will see a blank editor, and you must recall the program to retrieve the statements, for example, by pressing the F4 key. The Advanced Editor has many enhancements. It color codes the statements that you enter to help keep your program organized. For example, the DATA and PROC commands are in dark blue. Other SAS command statements or **keywords** are in light blue. Options, variable names, and other information on statements are in black. Data embedded in the program (as opposed to being read from an external data file) are highlighted in yellow.

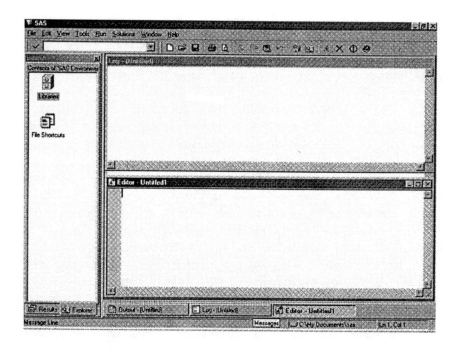

Figure 1.2. Illustration of the Windows 95/98/2000 SAS System Interface for SAS Release 8.01

Comment statements are in green. There is also limited error checking; if you misspell keywords, they will be highlighted in red. You must be careful about using both editors at the same time, as changes made in one will not necessarily show up in the other. When you press the F5 key you will be taken to the Program Editor rather than the Advanced Editor. The latter you can easily access with the buttons beneath the Editor window. You can use more than one editor at a time, which enables you to work with several programs simultaneously. Each will have its own button on the bottom. The two editors can be distinguished by a blue plus sign to the left of where it says Editor on the button at the bottom of the screen and on the top title bar of the Editor window.

The pulldown menus at the top of Figure 1.2 contain the commands you will need to run the SAS software interface. Although it is beyond our scope to cover them in detail, I will point out the most important. As is typical of most Windows software, under **F**ile you will find commands to open files, save files, and print. A very useful feature is *I*mport Data. This allows you to import several different kinds of data files into your SAS program, including EXCEL.

The next pulldown is **E**dit, which contains the commands to cut and paste part of your program in the Editor window. It also allows you to do find, and find and replace, functions. Keep in mind that the functions that will be available are determined by which window you are using. You can tell by the title bar of the window being blue, and by the window's button at the bottom of the screen being depressed. To the right of **E**dit is **V**iew, which can be used to skip from window to window. **Tools** and **S**olutions give you access to additional SAS features that won't be of concern in this book. Tools also allows you to customize many aspects of the SAS interface under **C**ustomize and **O**ptions. For example, **Options** lets you change the font and size of characters on the screen.

On the left-hand side of the menu bar is a white space, or **command bar**, where you can write commands (look to the right of the check mark in the upper left corner of Figure 1.2). You can click on the white space with your mouse or press the F11 key to put a cursor in the command bar so you can type a command. The command will work for whichever of the three windows you have active. From here you can enlarge the window by typing "zoom," or erase the window by typing "clear." The commands you type in the command bar will be saved, and you can use them by clicking on the little down arrowhead (upside-down triangle) just to the right of the command bar. To the right of the command bar are icons that you can use to do some of the most common tasks, such as open a file, save a file, run the program, and get help.

Running Program 1.1
With the Windows Version

Regardless of which version you use, you must enter your SAS program in a form that the computer can use. To run the sample Program 1.1, you must enter it into your computer system. So that you can reuse the program, you would give the file a name and store it somewhere (e.g., on hard drive or diskette). To run or execute the program, you must give the appropriate command. You can do this by pressing the F8 key, clicking on the toolbar icon of the person running (see in Figure 1.1 just below where it says "Window," or in Figure 1.2, third icon from the right), or by clicking on the **L**ocals pulldown menu (Release 6.11) or the **Run** pulldown (Release 8.01), and then on **Submit**. With other versions of the software for other types of computers, you might have to do this differently.

After your program has been executed, the results will show up in the output screen. From here you can review the results, and if you like, you can save them to a file or print them. Because the output can be quite large, I often save the output file, then use a word processor to condense it before printing. Release 6.11 did not allow editing in the Output window, but Release 8.01 does. The Log window will contain a listing of every SAS statement that was executed; information about every file from which data were input and to which data were output; information about the number of variables and cases that were processed; warning messages about various conditions encountered, such as missing data or invalid data (e.g., finding a letter where a number was expected); and error messages. It is always best to review the log first to be sure the program didn't have errors before looking at the output.

The SAS Log produced by Program 1.1 is shown as Log 1.1. As you can see, the log contains all the statements from Program 1.1 except the data itself. There are three Notes. The first one, about the lines written to the file, indicates that the PUT statement was executed one time. The second note says that the working data set (which will be discussed in Chapter 2) has one case or observation. The third note indicates how long it took for the program to execute. This log was taken from the Windows version of the SAS System. The exact contents of the log may vary from system to system.

Log 1.2 shows what happens when an error occurs within a SAS program. The program that was executed was the same as Program 1.1, except that in line 5, the statement PRINT was substituted for FILE PRINT. As you can see, the log listed all the SAS statements encountered. After statement 5, the incorrect statement PRINT is listed separately and underlined. Next a message is printed indicating that a "statement not valid or used out of proper order" was encountered. Note that the Log does not tell you how to correct this problem to accomplish what you wish to accomplish. It does indicate in this case, however, where it encountered the problem. Keep in mind that the line indicated is not always the real source of the problem, and often it lies elsewhere. In addition, one error can produce multiple error messages throughout your program, so the first error message encountered in a program is often the most important. Error messages provide hints that, with experience, you learn to interpret.

There are two Notes at the bottom of this log. The first tells you that processing was stopped because of the errors encountered. This is typically what

Log 1.1
The Log From Program 1.1

```
1      DATA TEST;
2         INPUT A B C D E;
3         TOTAL = A + B + C + D + E;
4         MEAN = TOTAL/5;
5         FILE PRINT;
6         PUT "MEAN = " MEAN;
7      Datalines;

NOTE: 1 lines were written to file PRINT.
NOTE: The data set WORK.TEST has 1
observations and 7 variables.
NOTE: The DATA statement used:
      real time 0.22 seconds.
8      ;
9      RUN;
```

happens when there is an error in a program. The second Note indicates the amount of time it took to execute the program. There are also two Warning messages. The first was that the data set was incomplete and there were no observations in the data set. Again this was caused by the fact that the program was halted due to an error. The second says that the data set was not replaced, which was also caused by the fact that the error halted completion of the execution.

You should carefully check the SAS Log from every program that you run. It contains important information that can help you determine if an error has been made.

How the SAS Log and program output are handled depends on the particular computer system. On some mainframes, the SAS Log and program output are mixed together. With most simple programs involving a single data step, the SAS Log comes first, followed by the program output. With the Windows version from which the examples here were taken, the log and output are displayed in different windows. Also, the exact nature of the messages and warnings can vary somewhat from one version of SAS to another.

Log 1.2
The Log From Program 1.1 With a Syntax Error

```
1     DATA TEST;
2        INPUT A B C D E;
3        TOTAL = A + B + C + D + E;
4        MEAN = TOTAL/5;
NOTE: SCL source line.
5     PRINT;
      ----
      180
ERROR 180-322: Statement is not valid or
it is used out of proper order.

6        PUT "MEAN = " MEAN;
7        Datalines;

NOTE: The SAS System stopped processing
this step because of errors.
WARNING: The data set WORK.TEST may be
incomplete. When this step was stopped
there were 0 observations and 7 variables.
WARNING: Data set WORK.TEST was not
replaced because this step was stopped.
NOTE: The DATA statement used:
         real time 0.38 seconds.
9     ;
10    RUN;
```

HOW TO APPROACH
PROGRAMMING A PROBLEM

The easiest way to write a program is to begin with some prior planning. It is much easier to write a program once its structure and major components have been sketched out or outlined. Particularly with long or complex programs, it is quicker and less frustrating if you lay out the structure of your program before you actually write out or enter the specific SAS statements. Typically you begin with a very general plan and then fill in details. Once you have the structure planned and know exactly what you want to accomplish, it is easier to fill in the program statements.

The first step in planning a program is exactly specifying the nature of the problem to be programmed. This involves writing down what you wish to accomplish, including the nature of the data to be inputted, the analyses and statistics to be conducted, the results to be outputted, and the format of the output. The more detail that is specified at this stage, the easier it will be to figure out the steps necessary to accomplish your objective. It is helpful at this stage to write out the format of the input files (if data are to be inputted from an external file). It is also helpful to sketch out what the output should look like.

For Program 1.1, the problem specification is quite simple. Its purpose is to input five numbers, calculate their mean, and produce a report that includes the value for the mean.

Once you have a clear picture of what you are trying to accomplish, you can figure out the major steps involved in your program. This can take the form of a flowchart, where you list the major tasks in order. Arrows indicate the order or flow of processing from task to task. An example of a flowchart for the simple example above is shown in Figure 1.3. It indicates that first the program will input the five observations. Next it will calculate the mean. Finally, the results will be outputted in a report. For a simple example like this one, the flowchart may seem of little value, but for complex programs it can be essential.

Another planning tool for programs is to write out the major statements for a program in what is called **pseudocode**. Whereas a flowchart contains the major components of a program, it does not specify specific statements. Pseudocode provides much greater detail by writing down the major statements, not necessarily in proper SAS format. Thus it is a step halfway between the flowchart and the actual program. Particularly for the inexperienced programmer, it will be easier to write out the step-by-step instructions in pseudocode first. You can focus entirely on the logical flow of the program without being concerned with the form of the SAS statements. As you become more experienced with the SAS language, you may find that a detailed flowchart is enough of a guide when you sit down to write a program.

Table 1.2 contains an example of pseudocode. As you can see, it is more detailed than the flowchart in Figure 1.1. Each line of the table represents one or two statements from the SAS program. Some of the statements have parts that look a bit like SAS statements, for example, the third and fourth statements,

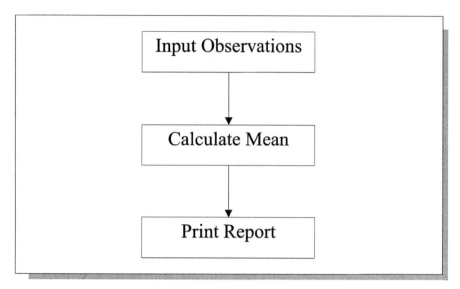

Figure 1.3. Flowchart of a Program to Compute the Mean of Five Numbers

which do the calculations contain, SAS expressions. From this pseudocode, it would be quite easy to write a SAS program.

DEBUGGING A PROGRAM

Even for the most experienced programmer, it is rare to write a program that runs correctly the first time. Perhaps the most difficult thing for the novice programmer to accept is that programming is an iterative process of writing and debugging. You write a program and run it. You fix errors that have occurred and run the program again. You fix more errors and run the program again. This process continues until you are confident that the program is running properly.

Commercial software companies will sometimes have thousands of people try out a program to find out if it has logical errors or bugs. The total time devoted to testing and debugging a program can sometimes be greater than the time spent writing it. Testing and debugging is a vital step in programming. A single misplaced letter, number, or punctuation mark can completely change what a program does. It is almost impossible to have everything absolutely

---

Table 1.2

Pseudocode for a Program to Compute the Mean of Five Numbers

```
Name data set = Test
Input five variables A, B, C, D, E
Calculate Total = A+B+C+D+E
Calculate Mean = Total/5
Print report, MEAN = __
```

---

correct the first time for any but the smallest and simplest programs. Once the program is written, the job is only half done. It still must be tested and debugged to be sure it is running properly. This often will take many test runs, and it isn't unusual to run even a simple program dozens of times to debug it completely.

The most frustrating aspect of programming for most people is debugging. You will enjoy programming a great deal more if you accept the fact that making errors is an integral part of the programming process. Don't think of your errors as a reflection on your lack of skill or experience. Every programmer makes both syntax and logical errors. Instead consider the debugging of a program as a challenge, much like the solving of a puzzle. You should find that the more challenging the problem, the bigger the sense of satisfaction you will have when you solve it!

Types of Errors

There are two major categories of errors with which you must contend. The first are the SAS **syntax errors**. These are like errors of grammar, where your instruction does not have the proper form or the instructions conflict with one another, or of vocabulary, where you use the wrong name for a statement or you misspell it. This can occur if you use the wrong word for the name of a statement (e.g., INPUTTING rather than INPUT) or misspell a statement INPUR rather than INPUT). It can happen if you put something in the statement that is not understood. For example, multiplication is indicated by an asterisk, "*".

You cannot use an "x" (e.g., PRODUCT = A x B). You must also be careful that everything in every statement is in agreement.

The other type of error is a **logical error**. This is when your statement is understood by the computer, but the statement does not accomplish what you intended. With Program 1.1, the statement

```
TOTAL = A * B * C * D * E;
```

specifies the product and not the sum of the five variables. If the sum was intended, this statement would produce a logical error. The computer will not know the difference because this is a valid SAS statement.

The SAS System will automatically tell you when there is a SAS syntax error. All such errors are listed in the SAS Log. These error messages are generally quite cryptic and often merely give you clues about what might be wrong. Logical errors are more difficult to detect because SAS will give you no indication that anything is wrong. You must find logical errors by conducting tests of your program to make sure it is doing what you intend.

Finding Errors

The best way to approach debugging is to be systematic and thorough. Do the best job you can in getting the program written correctly, realizing it is very likely there will be some mistakes that arise from typographical errors, inadvertent omissions, logical errors, and misconceptions about the SAS language. You might think of the initial writing of a program as similar to the first draft of a paper that must be checked for errors and polished into a final draft.

Once the program is written you should run it and first look for syntax errors in the SAS Log, where they will indicate syntax errors and logical inconsistencies across statements. Note that with SAS Release 8.01 there are some syntax checks built into the Program Editor that will work much like an online spellchecker with a word processor. It will tell you when you have made an error that you can fix immediately. Syntax errors should be fixed and then the program rerun and the Log rechecked, as sometimes it can take several iterations of fixing errors and resubmitting until the SAS Log ceases to give error messages and warnings. Because sometimes a single error can cause multiple error messages, sometimes it can be efficient to fix errors sequentially one by one from the first one encountered, rerunning the program iteratively and checking the log after fixing each error.

Perhaps the most common cause of a syntax error is forgetting to put a semicolon ";" at the end of a statement. This is the first thing you should look for when you see an error has occurred. Be aware that the error message does not always indicate the line where the error actually occurred, so look at all the statements above the one with the Log error message to be sure there are no missing semicolons. If there are no missing semicolons, then the statement indicated as in error should be closely examined to see if its syntax is correct. The error messages themselves will provide hints about what might be wrong.

Logical errors can be far more difficult to detect and correct. Because the computer doesn't know that an error has been made, it will give you no hints that something is wrong. To be certain that your program is working correctly, you must test it in situations where you know the correct answer. Resist the temptation to stop your debugging efforts after the syntax errors are fixed. There can still be serious errors that will prevent your program from doing what you intend.

To check for logical errors, you must run a series of diagnostic tests. With Program 1.1, for example, you would calculate the mean by hand and compare your answer with the program's. For more complex problems, it might be possible to enter a problem that someone has already solved. Often a statistics book will provide a worked out example. A complex program that may allow for many optional procedures and combinations of procedures may require extensive work to test all its possibilities. You might have to test a series of problems with known solutions to be sure the program is functioning properly.

For a difficult problem, a good approach is to build the program step by step, in stages. Each stage can be tested to make sure it operates properly before the next stage is added. This is particularly important when you are attempting to program a task that you have never done before. It can be much easier to work with one small section of a program rather than an entire program. Sometimes a piece of a program should be developed separately and then incorporated into the full program.

As we cover various programming features, some advice and hints about debugging will be given. In the following chapter we will cover ways that you can output results of your SAS program and how this output can be used to test your program.

SAS STATEMENTS

Instructions that you write must be stated properly according to the SAS language, using **SAS statements**. A SAS statement is a command or instruction that is written in a way that will be interpreted correctly by the SAS System. There can be more than one way to specify what you wish the SAS System to do, but the number of equivalent SAS statements is quite limited. Not only must you learn what each SAS statement does, but you must learn its proper form or **syntax**. Appendix B is a summary of the SAS language statements used in this book.

There is one hard and fast rule for SAS statements: Each must end in a semicolon ";". The semicolon is how the computer knows that a statement is over. You can see in Program 1.1 that every SAS statement ended in a semicolon. The only exception in the example was for the data lines, which are not SAS statements. There is another exception within a SAS program, and that is for labels, which will be covered in Chapter 5. Perhaps the biggest cause of SAS syntax errors is the omission of a semicolon at the end of a statement. Often this results in an error, not in the statement without the semicolon, but in a later statement. This is because the statement without the semicolon and the following statement are treated as a single statement. This can cause an error not only at this place in the program but also in later places. A good strategy is to check first for missing semicolons when you find a syntax error in the SAS Log.

Another feature of the SAS language is that you can insert comments within the program. A comment is a message you put within the program that is not an instruction to be executed. Comments can be used as notes to yourself throughout the program to remind you what the various statements are doing. In a long program, it is difficult to remember the function of every statement. Comments help you keep track of what various portions of the program are doing. They also help organize the program. This makes it easier, both with the initial program development and with later debugging, testing, and modifications. Comments are also very helpful to someone else who may wish to modify your program in the future.

Comments are also useful at the beginning of a program to describe what the program is intended to accomplish. They can include any special instructions, such as the form of the data to be inputted or the optional things the program might do. This is particularly helpful when you have written many programs and you don't remember which program does which thing. From my experience, it doesn't take you very long to forget what a program is supposed to do.

Comments can begin with an asterisk "*" and end with a semicolon, or they can be sandwiched between two slash-asterisks "/*". They can take up part of one line or several lines. They can be placed at the end of each line. Program 1.2 is Program 1.1 with comments added that show both forms of the comments. In this case, the comments are all placed at the right-hand side of the program lines. In later examples in this book, comments will be placed on their own lines.

In this case, there is a comment after every SAS program statement, except for the DATALINES statement and data, where they should not be placed. The comments indicate what each statement is designed to accomplish. For example, the first statement names the data step, the second statement inputs the five variables, and so on. Of course, with a simple program like this one, it hardly seems worthwhile to add comments. For a long or complex program, however, it is easier to refer to a comment about what the program is doing at a particular place than to trace through the SAS statements to figure out what is happening.

ADDITIONAL HELP

The SAS language is very extensive, with hundreds of built-in features, statements, and functions. Many of the features are highly specialized and will be of use to relatively few programmers. Others are used in almost every program written. It would be beyond the scope of this introductory book to cover every feature of the SAS language. This book will cover the major features that should be sufficient for most uses. In many places the treatment of the possible functions of a statement will be incomplete. Usually, the first place to go for information is the online help if your version of SAS has it. With the Windows version, the syntax for all commands and PROCs are in the help file that can be accessed by pressing the F1 key, by clicking on the help icon (book with a question mark) on the taskbar, or by clicking on the **Help** pulldown menu. Some university (and other organization) facilities have online versions of SAS System manuals on their Web sites that are accessible to those with a password. Even more details can be found in the books and manuals that are available from the SAS Institute. This material is also available on the SAS

Program 1.2
Example of a SAS® Program With Comments

```
1  DATA TEST;                        *Name data step;
2  INPUT A B C D E;                  /*Input five variables/*
3  TOTAL = A + B + C + D + E;        *Sum the data;
4  MEAN = TOTAL/5;                   *Compute the mean;
5  FILE PRINT;                       *Print report;
6  PUT "MEAN = " MEAN;               *Format the output;
7  DATALINES;
8  1 2 3 4 5
9  ;
10 RUN;
```

OnlineDoc Version 8 CD-ROM that contains PDF format files of many manuals. Another good source of information is the SAS Institute Web site, http://www.sas.com.

For a complete reference to the SAS language itself, the best source is the language reference for Release 6, *SAS® Language: Reference, Version 6, First Edition* (1990); for Release 8, *SAS® Language Reference: Dictionary Version 8, Volumes 1 and 2* (1999). This manual is extremely thorough in covering the details of the SAS language. Whereas the current book covers the basics of each statement, this manual gives the details. If you are using the Windows version of SAS, you may find *SAS® Companion for Microsoft Windows Environment Version 8* (1999) of interest. For documentation on the statistical procedures or PROCs, there are manuals for Release 6, *SAS/STAT® User's Guide, Version 6, Fourth Edition, Volumes 1 and 2* (1989); for Release 8 *SAS/STAT® User's Guide, Version 8, Fourth Edition, Volumes 1-3* (1999). Many other books and manuals are available from the SAS Institute Inc. A partial list of books that might be of interest is in Appendix D of this book.

Another source of help can be experienced SAS programmers (e.g., your instructor if you are taking a SAS course) whom you might consult when you get really stumped. Use such people only as absolutely necessary. If you ask someone else to fix all your errors, it will impede your learning how to program and/or debug. It may be useful to have someone help you occasionally, and you may learn a great deal from him or her. If you use the person as a crutch, however, your development as a SAS programmer will be curtailed.

USING THIS BOOK

The remainder of this book will be a step-by-step guide to programming with the SAS language. Chapters 2-8 will cover the various programming features necessary for the analysis of data with the SAS language. Features will be covered to input, manipulate, and output information. These chapters will cover the basics, which you will be able to utilize in writing your own programs. Chapter 9 covers five PROCs that accomplish simple statistical analyses.

The best way to use this book is in conjunction with the SAS System itself. Enter the examples on your computer system and run them. Once they run properly, make modifications and see what happens. See if you can embellish the programs. With Program 1.1, see what happens if you add an additional line of data. Add another variable to the input line and add another number to the data line. Don't forget to change the sample size to 6 in the denominator of the mean formula. In short, don't be afraid to play with the programs. Through experimentation and experience, you will gain skill in the SAS language. You may be surprised that in a relatively short time you can write sophisticated programs to solve your data analysis problems.

Another feature of the book that will help you develop your skill is the debugging exercises in Chapters 1-8. Each exercise is a simple program that has errors. The best way to use this feature is to enter the program into your SAS editor as written, and run it. See what error messages, if any, you get in the Log. See what output it produced, and see if it looks correct. Then fix the errors. Some you may notice as you enter the program, and others you may have to figure out through a process of elimination. If you get stuck, Appendix E will give some hints about what's wrong.

Keep in mind that programming is a skill, much like playing golf or tennis. The only way to really learn is to practice. A book can give you an overview and explain the features, but you must write your own programs to acquire the skill. Reading alone is not enough.

Available on my Web site (http://chuma.cas.usf.edu/~Spector) are some online resources to help you learn SAS programming. On the main page, click on the title of this book. I teach an online SAS course, and this course is on the site to be used by individual students in self-study, or by an instructor of a SAS course. The site contains some SAS projects that can be used in conjunction with the book, as well as links and supplemental information. I also have some practice data sets available. You will find a description of each data set and the format. They all contain real data that are not contrived examples.

∾ Debugging Exercises ∾

For this chapter, the debugging exercises involve Program 1.1. Errors have been added to each program. Without looking back at the original, try to figure out what's wrong. The best way to do this is to enter the program into your SAS Editor, run it, and then try to figure out what's wrong. Hints can be found in Appendix E.

Exercise 1.1

```
INPUT A B C D;
TOTAL = A + B + C + D + E;
MEAN = TOTAL/5;
FILE PRINT;
PUT 'MEAN = ' MEAN;
DATALINES;
1 2 3 4 5
;
RUN;
```

Exercise 1.2

```
INPUT A B C D E;
TOTAL = A + B + C + D + E;
MEAN = TOTAL/5;
FILE PRINT;
PUT 'MEAN = ' MEAN;
DATALINES;
1 2 3 4 5;
;
RUN;
```

Chapter *2*

Inputting and Outputting Data

The SAS language programs we will discuss in this book have as their major purpose the manipulation and analysis of data. In order to manipulate data, you must first instruct the computer to input them. Once data are inputted and manipulated, the results are output in some form so that they can be used. With the Windows version of the SAS System, results will automatically go to the output window, where you can view them.

A common programming task is to analyze the results of a survey. Suppose you have a data file that contains survey data from a national sample of registered voters. Included might be responses to questions concerning attitudes about individual candidates and respondents' intentions to vote for particular candidates. A SAS program can be written to input the data from the file, prepare it for analysis, conduct the analysis, and output the results in a report. Preparations might include the combining of individual items into total scores, or the handling of missing data. It might also be of interest to output subsets of the original file. For example, you might wish to create one data set of Republicans and another of Democrats for use later.

Within the SAS language, inputting, manipulation, and some outputting are done within the **data step**. A data step is a series of program statements that accomplishes a particular series of tasks. A data step begins with a DATA statement and ends when a CARDS, DATALINES, PROC, or another DATA statement is encountered, or when the last program statement has been executed. In Program 1.1 there was a single data step that began with the first line (DATA TEST) and ended with the sixth line, containing the PUT statement.

One of the activities that occurs within a data step is that one or more SAS data sets are built. These SAS data sets can be "working" data sets that will exist only while the particular program is executing. Alternately, they can be saved permanently in a SAS data library. These libraries contain not only the data but the names of the variables as well. They can be easier to work with than the original data files because the inputting, variable naming, and manipulating of data have already been done.

SAS working data sets have two purposes. First, to analyze data with a SAS PROC, the data must first be placed in a SAS working data set. The data step inputs the data and accomplishes any manipulations necessary for the analysis to be done by the PROCs. The second purpose is that a SAS data set can be input directly into another data step without having to define all the variables again in the second data set. This second purpose will be discussed at length in this chapter.

DEFINING A DATA SET

As you saw in Program 1.1 in Chapter 1, a data step begins with a DATA statement. The DATA statement has two purposes. First, it gives a name to the particular SAS data set or sets that will be created by the data step. This becomes important when there are several data steps in the same program. The other purpose is that the DATA statement can tell SAS to output data to a SAS data library for permanent storage.

The name you give the data step depends upon whether it will be a temporary SAS working data set or a SAS data library data set. For a SAS working data set, the name can be any combination of up to 32 (8 for Release 6.x) characters (letters, numbers, and underscores, "_"), but the first character must be a letter or underscore. Thus A335B is a valid name, but 2FILE is not because it begins with a number, 2. Rules for a SAS data library data set will be discussed later.

If you fail to specify a data set name, one will be assigned automatically. The first data set in your program will be called DATA1, the second DATA2,

Table 2.1
Example of a Data File

```
 1 2 3 44 4 344 59 5
 2 4 8 48 7 154 12 9
 3 7 7 22 6 187 54 5
 4 3 8 71 2 253 17 4
 5 2 2 62 1 250 43 5
 6 1 8 32 8 478 40 8
 7 4 8 75 1 567 58 7
 8 8 3 37 2 484 76 5
 9 2 4 72 3 557 26 5
10 8 2 51 5 247 30 2
```

and so on. It is best to give names to data sets that describe their purpose; for example, CENSUS might be the name of a data set that contains census data.

Each data step creates at least one SAS data set. To understand how data are handled within the data step, you must understand the structure of a data file. Data in a computer file are usually organized into a matrix. That is, the numbers are placed into rows and columns. For each subject or case, there are data for one or more variables. To make sense, cases should be assessed on the same variables, although not every case has to have data on every variable. Table 2.1 is an example of a data file. There are 10 rows in the data file, representing 10 cases. For each case, there are eight separate variables assessed. The first variable is always found in the first two columns, the second variable is always in the fourth column, the third variable is in the sixth column, and so on. The first case had a value of 1 for the first variable, 2 for the second, 3 for the third, 44 for the fourth, and so on.

Although it is possible to make each row of a data file as long as you would like, it is convenient to limit row length to what can be displayed across one line on your computer monitor. The original convention was to limit row length to no more than 80 columns or numbers because this was the number of columns on a computer card. The convention continued after cards became obsolete because 80 was the number of characters that could be displayed in a line on a monitor screen. In the Windows environment it is possible to have more than 80 characters, so you can set line length to be longer, depending on your monitor size and the font you use. It is most convenient, however, to make sure you can see an entire line on the screen without having to shift the screen back and forth. This is also true for the program editor window where you write your program and for the output window where the results are displayed. Line length for the program editor is set within the SAS Program Interface as an option. Line length for output can be set with an option command at the beginning of your SAS program, as discussed later.

Individual cases are not limited to a single line of data in the data file. Suppose you gave a five-choice, 160-item multiple-choice test to a sample of subjects. With 80-character rows, it would take two rows to hold all 160 responses. The first 80 items would be in the first row, and the second 80 items would be in the second. The appropriate SAS statement would be used to assign all 160 items to the proper case for analysis.

The data step itself allows you to input a data set such as the one in Table 2.1. It then converts it into a SAS data set, which contains not only the data in the file but also information about variable names and a listing of the SAS program that created it. Although the original data file can be displayed on your computer screen using a text editor (e.g., the SAS program editor) or a word processor, a SAS data set cannot be viewed directly. PROC PRINT can be used to see what is in the SAS data set. This PROC will be discussed later in this chapter. A note in the SAS Log indicates the number of cases and variables in each SAS data set in a program.

The data set created within the data step can be used by other data steps within your SAS program, or it can be output to a permanent storage location such as a diskette, hard drive, CD, or Zip disk. The first use will be illustrated later in this chapter. Permanent storage of SAS data sets will be covered in Chapter 8.

The data step itself is used to build a data set. It begins with the data that you enter, which is organized into variables. Each variable (in Table 2.1 there are eight) is given a name and is referred to within the data step by that name. You can do all sorts of manipulations to the variables that you enter, including changing the values of the variables, creating new variables, and adding and deleting cases or variables. When the entire data step has been executed, the data set created will contain the data after all manipulations, additions, and deletions have been accomplished.

You can have multiple data steps within a single SAS program. Program 2.1 is an example with multiple data steps. As you can see, there are two

---

Program 2.1
Examples of Inputting and Outputting

```
 1 *This Data Step Copies Data from a File
on Disk to the Print
 2  Location (Screen or Printer);
 3 DATA CRIME;
 4  INFILE 'A:CRIME.DAT';
 5  INPUT CRIMERAT 3. UNEMP 2.1 EDUC 4.;
 6  FILE PRINT;
 7  PUT 'Crime = ' CRIMERAT
 8  @15 'Unemployment = ' UNEMP
 9  @35 'State per pupil expenditure = $'
EDUC;
 10 PROC PRINT;
 11 *This Data Step Inputs the SAS Data Set
CRIME and Outputs Each Case Twice Into Data
Set "Two";
 12 DATA TWO;
 13 SET CRIME;
 14 OUTPUT;
 15 OUTPUT;
 16 PROC PRINT;
 17 RUN;
```

DATA statements that create two SAS data sets named CRIME and TWO. For TWO, data were inputted from the prior SAS data set CRIME.

LOCATION OF THE
DATA SET TO INPUT

To input data into a SAS data step, you must use a statement to indicate where those data are. There are three possibilities for data location. Data can be placed inside the program at the end of the data step, they can be in a file outside your SAS program, or they can be in a SAS data library.

Inside the Program

Program 1.1 from Chapter 1 illustrates how data can be entered inside a SAS program, at the end of the data step statements. To indicate that the data are inside your SAS program, you must use a DATALINES (or CARDS—they are interchangeable) statement. Data must begin on a new line of the file, immediately following the DATALINES statement. The line following the last line of data must be a semicolon. Thus, data lines are placed between DATALINES and the semicolon. The DATALINES statement must follow all other statements within your data step, as it signals that the data step has ended. Any PROC statements to be used with the data step must follow the DATALINES and data.

Program 1.1 shows the correct way to put data inside a data step. The following

```
DATALINES;  1  2  3  2  3  3;
```

is incorrect because the data are on the same line as the DATALINES statement. The semicolon that signifies the end of the data must be on a new line. The correct form is

```
DATALINES;
1  2  3  2  3  3
;
```

External File

A more common way to input data is to put them in a data file outside your SAS program on diskette, hard drive, or other storage device (e.g., CD or Zip disk). Such files must be in a format that can be read by a SAS program. On a PC this means the data must be in ASCII (text) format. On other kinds of computers, the format might differ.

The statement to input an external file is the INFILE statement. With the PC versions of SAS, you specify the name and location of the file. With other kinds of computers, the way you note the file name might differ.

The first data step in Program 2.1 uses an INFILE statement to input a data set named A:CRIME.DAT, which on a PC would be located on a diskette in floppy drive "A." The proper form of the statement is the word FILE, followed by a space, and then the name of the file placed in single quotes. On a PC, the drive letter should be specified. Examples of INFILE statements are

```
INFILE 'A:MYDAT';
INFILE 'C:DATINP';
INFILE 'C:\SASPROG\PROJECT\CENSUS';
```

SAS Data Library

The final possible location for a data set is in a SAS data library. The contents of a SAS data set created by a data step can be outputted and saved permanently on diskette, hard drive, or other storage device. Such library files contain not only the numbers but also the variable names, programs that created them, and other technical information. They are useful for situations where you wish to manipulate "raw data" before analysis. For example, you might wish to combine individual observations into some total scores and then analyze the total scores. In some applications totals might be the sum or mean of thousands of individual observations. The scoring program need not be run each time an analysis of total scores is conducted, but rather the totals can be taken from the SAS library file. For large, complex programs, this can be a very efficient way to work.

Each data step creates one or more SAS working data sets. These data sets exist only while the program is executing and disappear when the program is finished. You can input any prior data set into a later data step. The procedure is similar if you are reading data from a SAS data library data set.

To input a SAS data set, use the SET statement. For prior data sets within a single program, you merely give the data set name. The form of the statement is SET, space, and name of the data set. The second data step in Program 2.1 uses the SET statement

```
SET CRIME;
```

to input data from the SAS data set created by the first data step.

For an external SAS data library data set, you must add the library name to the file name, using the form "library name.file name". There will be a library name and file name separated by a period. The exact form of the library name will vary across releases and versions of SAS. See Chapter 8 for a more extensive treatment of SAS data libraries.

INPUTTING DATA LINES

A characteristic of the SAS language is that it processes data one **case** at a time. This is very useful for statistical data analysis, where you typically take one or more observations on one or more separate sampling units. These **sampling units**, or cases, in the social sciences, usually are individual people or groups of people, but they could be other things such as animals, countries, states, or time periods. Within the data step each case is entered one by one, and data manipulation is done on each case in order. In other words, every time a case is input, the statements in the data step are executed one by one until the end of the data step is encountered. Execution then returns to the beginning of the data step, another case is input, and the statements are executed again. This continues until all cases have been inputted.

This method of processing case by case is different from most other computer languages, which allow you to enter all cases simultaneously and operate on them at the same time. This case-by-case processing makes it easier to program some problems with the SAS language, and it makes it more difficult to program others. For statistical data analysis, however, this sort of processing usually simplifies programming. This is why the SAS System is the language of choice for many statistical and other data analysis problems.

When inputting data using the DATALINES (CARDS) or FILE statement, you must name all the variables and indicate their location within the file. This can be done with the INPUT statement. With SAS data sets, on the other hand, the variable names and file locations are handled directly by the SAS System, so you can't use an INPUT statement.

The INPUT statement directs the computer to enter a case and assigns the variable names to the data that are in specified locations. A case can have all its data on a single data line of the file, or it can be spread over several contiguous lines.

As you can see in Table 2.1, each variable is organized in its own column or columns. For illustrative purposes, spaces were skipped between variables, but this is unnecessary. Within the INPUT statement, each variable must be given a name, and its location within the data line must be specified. This is done by numbering the columns from left to right beginning with column 1. As you can see in Table 2.1, the first variable ranges from 1 to 10. Thus it takes two digits to represent every possibility. Note that there is a blank space before each single digit number one to nine. This is called *right justification* and is necessary when you are specifying column positions for variable input. The first variable occupies columns 1 and 2 of each data line. Hence you specify its location as being in these two columns. The second variable has a single digit and is located in column 4, the third variable is in column 6, and so on.

Specifying Column Locations

The SAS language allows several options for how you specify column locations for variables. Perhaps the easiest option is to specify the column number or numbers. Thus, an INPUT statement for the file in Table 2.1 would be

```
INPUT ID 1-2 Var1 4 Var2 6 Var3 8-9 Var4 11 Var5 13-15
Var6 17-18 Var7 20;
```

On this INPUT statement, the first variable is given the name ID. The remaining variables are given the name Var, plus a number from 1 to 7. You can give each variable a different letter name, or the same letter name with different numbers. You must be careful that two variables do not have names with all characters the same. Variable names can be from 1 to 32 (8 for Release 6.x) characters long. A name must begin with a letter or an underscore ("_"). The remaining characters can be letters, numbers, or underscores. The numbers following each name are the column locations for each variable. Thus, ID can be found in columns 1 and 2, Var1 is in column 4, Var2 is in column 6, and so on.

W.d Formats

Another style of specification is to indicate the format for each variable, rather than its column location. This is particularly useful for data sets that have no blank spaces between variables. Each time a new data line is begun, inputting begins in the leftmost column or column 1. The column presently being read is referred to as the **pointer location**. As a data line is input, the pointer moves across the line from variable to variable, moving the number of spaces specified for each variable.

In the present example, the first variable, ID, occupies columns 1 and 2. You can specify two columns for ID with the following:

```
INPUT ID 2.
```

The "2." indicates that ID is two digits long and occupies two columns. Because ID was the first variable specified on the INPUT statement, the pointer begins in column 1 and reads two columns (1 and 2). Thus, you don't have to specify column locations.

The second variable is in column 4, but the pointer is in column 3. You give an instruction to move the pointer one column with a "+1", as in

```
INPUT ID 2. +1 VAR1 1.
```

You can also give an instruction to move the pointer to column 4 with an "@4," as in

```
INPUT ID 2. @4 VAR1 1.
```

In both cases, the "1." tells SAS that the variable VAR1 is one digit long. Now the pointer is at column 5. You can use the @ or + to skip to column 6, where VAR2 is read with another "1.".

With this input style, you can read in numbers that have decimal components by specifying the number of digits to the right of the decimal. The general form is W.d, where W refers to the total number of digits and d refers to the number to the right of the decimal. If you were to read ID with a 2.1, this would in effect divide all ID values by 10. That is, the first case would have a value of .1 rather than 1, the second would be .2 rather than 2, and so on. If you used a 2.2 format, the first case would be .01, the second, .02, the third, .03, and so on. If d is greater than W, leading zeros will be inserted. For example, the first case read with a 2.5 format would be equal to .00001.

There is a shortcut way to input several variables that occupy the same number of columns. For example, suppose you have 10 observations on each case, and each observation occupies one column. They should be entered with no spaces between them. Suppose the 10 items occupy columns 1 to 10. You can use the following shortcut statement to input them:

```
INPUT (X1-X10) (1.);
```

This statement specifies the names and locations for all 10 variables at once. They must all have the same variable name, X, with the different variables distinguished only by the subscript number 1 to 10. The parentheses are necessary. The above statement is equivalent to the following:

```
INPUT X1 1. X2 1. X3 1. X4 1. X5 1. X6 1. X7 1. X8 1. X9
1. X10 1.;
```

When a case occupies more than a single line in a data file, you can skip to another line with the "/" symbol or to a specified line number with the "#n" statement, where *n* is the line number of interest. The following statements:

```
INPUT ID 10. (X1-X60) (1.) / (X61-X120) (1.);
INPUT ID 10. (X1-X60) (1.) #2 (X61-X120) (1.);
```

both input the variables ID and X1 through X60 from the first line. They then skip to the second line to read in X61 to X120. In the first case, the instruction is to skip to the next line. In the second case, the instruction is to skip to the second line. You must be careful with multiple lines (there is no limit to their number) that all cases have the same number of lines. With this example, it is presumed that every other line begins a new case. If a case is missing a line, the inputting will be off one line for every following case. If data were missing for variables X61 to X120, a blank line should be used as a placeholder. With the PC version, be careful that the line contains 60 blank spaces (hit the spacebar 60 times), or better still, enter 60 periods (".") to indicate missing values; otherwise, the line may be ignored and the following line may be read by mistake. To guard against this possibility, be sure to put the MISSOVER option on the INFILE statement. Normally if there are missing variables, the SAS System will read onto the following line to find them rather than realize they are missing. MISSOVER says that when variables are missing from a line, do not read onto the next line, but rather count the variables as missing.

Character Values

So far situations have been considered where variables take on only numeric values. A SAS program can also work with variables that take on nonnumeric or alphabetic or character values as well as numeric values. This allows you to manipulate strings of text, such as people's names or addresses. Each character variable is limited to a length of 200 characters. The inputting procedures discussed so far indicate that the variables can only have numeric values. To specify character values, you put the appropriate designation on the INPUT statement.

With the W.d format, this involves putting a "$" before the W, as in

```
INPUT ID 2. NAME $18.;
```

The "$" indicates that nonnumeric values are allowable for the variable NAME. If you do not use the "$" and a variable has an alphabetic value, such as "f" or "G", an error message will be output to the SAS Log.

With the column location indicator, the "$" is placed before the column indication. There must be a blank space before and after the "$", as in

```
INPUT ID 1-2 NAME $ 3-20;
```

List Input

The type of inputting discussed so far is termed *fixed format* because each variable is in a fixed location on a data line. It is possible to use a free format, where locations are not fixed within each data line, which is termed *list input*. Delimiter characters are used to separate variables, which can be in any columns. A blank space is recognized as a delimiter that indicates when each variable has ended. The file in Table 2.1 is set up with a blank space between

variables, allowing it to be list inputted. To do this, eliminate the column locations on the INPUT statement and list the variables' names, for example:

```
INPUT ID VAR1 VAR2 VAR3 VAR4 VAR5 VAR6 VAR7;
```

Observations will be input to the variables in this order. Thus, the first observation encountered will be the ID, the second will be Var1, the third will be Var2,
and so on. The only restriction is that the variables must be in this order for
every case.

You can change the delimiter used by adding the DELIMITER= option to the
INFILE statement when entering data from an external file. For example,

```
INFILE 'a:mydata' DELIMITER = ",";
```

says to use commas as delimiters. This can be quite useful because some files
uses commas to delimit variables. For example, one of the optional output file
formats for EXCEL files is a comma-delimited file. It is possible to convert the
data in a spreadsheet to this kind of file that can then be input into a SAS program.
Because these files can produce very long line lengths, it is often necessary to
also add the LRECL= option to the INFILE statement, such as

```
INFILE 'a:mydata' LRECL = 800 DELIMITER = ",";
```

This allows for a line length of 800. A careful inspection of the SAS Log will
give an indication that the line length was too long and should be increased.
This will be seen in notes saying that data lines were truncated and that SAS
went to a new line when input reached past the end of a line. Either one of
these error messages is a clear indication that your data were not input
properly.

One must be careful about missing data with list input. If blanks are used as
the delimiter, the missing value will be seen as a delimiter and the following
variable will be erroneously assigned to the former variable. The safest way to
deal with this is to be sure missing variables are indicated with a period ("."). A
series of blanks will be read as one delimiter, not several. If you use comma
delimiters, just add an extra comma and blank (which is necessary) for the
missing value, as in "12, ,18." Do not forget the blank after the comma;
"CO12,,18" is incorrect.

Holding the Input Line

Each time an INPUT statement is executed, a new line is read from the data file. For example, suppose you wished to input the following data representing four variables assessed on each of three cases:

```
DATALINES;
1 2 3 2
2 1 3 2
3 3 2 1
;
```

Within the data step you would have an INPUT statement that indicated how each case is to be read. On each iteration of the data step, the INPUT statement would begin on a new data line. You do not have to indicate that the next case begins on a new line, because this is done automatically.

There are times, however, when you might want to override the automatic line skipping. This might occur because you are using two different INPUT statements to input your data, depending on the value of a variable for a case. To indicate that the line skipping should not be done, use the trailing "@" at the end of the INPUT statement. The statement

```
INPUT ID 2. @;
```

says to read the variable ID from the first two columns of each data line. The trailing @ says not to skip to the next line yet. Suppose that for the cases with ID less than 50, a variable of interest is in column 10, and if ID is equal to 50 or greater, the variable is in column 15. Using features not yet discussed, you can instruct the computer to use

```
INPUT VAR 10;
```

in the former case and

```
INPUT VAR 15;
```

Table 2.2
Variable Formats

General Form	Example	Description
a-b	1-3	Numeric variable occupies columns 1 to 3
$ a-b	$ 1-3	Character variable occupies columns 1 to 3
W.d	5.2	Numeric variable with 5 digits 2 to the right of the decimal
$W	$15.	Character variable with 15 characters
+n	+5	Skip 5 columns (spaces) within a data line
@n	@10	Skip to column 10 of the data line
/	/	Skip to the next data line
#n	#3	Skip to the third data line of the case
@(trailing)	@	Hold the current pointer position until the next case

in the latter. Without the trailing @, you would input ID from one case and the value of VAR from the following case. When the end of the data step is encountered for a particular iteration, the trailing @ is released, and the next data line will automatically be input. Thus, each time the first INPUT statement is executed, a new case will be inputted.

The various format instructions that can be used on an INPUT statement are summarized in Table 2.2. The table indicates the general form for each instruction, an example of the instruction, and the description of what the example indicates.

CONTROLLING OUTPUT
TO THE SAS DATA SET

Unless you specify otherwise, a SAS program will output each case into the SAS data set or sets that are created by the data step. One way to control the outputting of the cases is with the OUTPUT statement. Each time the OUTPUT statement is executed, the data step will output the present case to the SAS data set. This allows you to output some cases and not others.

Any manipulation of data within a case that occurs after the OUTPUT statement will not be output to the SAS data set. If you have more than one OUTPUT statement, the same case may be output to the SAS data set more than once. Program 2.1 contains a data step that uses the OUTPUT statement. It will be discussed later in this chapter.

SPECIFYING THE LOCATION FOR OUTPUTTING

Depending upon your computer system, you can direct the output of your data step to the screen, a diskette, a hard drive, a printer, or another storage device. The way you indicate where to send output is with the FILE statement. As with inputting, your specific system will determine exactly how you specify output file locations. With the Windows versions, if you specify the PRINT location, output will go to the Output Window.

If you wish to direct output to a specific file, you must give its file name. With the Windows version, this is done in the same way that you specify a file on an INFILE statement; that is, you indicate the drive letter, a colon, and the file name, all within single quotes, as

```
FILE 'a:mydat';
```

or

```
FILE 'c:\storage\datout.dat';
```

The first data step in Program 2.1 used a FILE statement (line 6) with a PRINT location to output to the Output Window. If a file name were substituted for PRINT, output would have been sent to a file. The rules for file naming are dictated by your computer system. With the Windows 98 versions of SAS, output file names must conform to the Windows convention. There can be from 1 to 255 characters in a file name, but the following characters are not allowed:

```
\ / : * ? " "  |
```

The following are all valid file names:

```
INPUT.DAT1992CENSUSDATA.INP
SURVEYDATAFROMSURVEY4
MY_DATA
```

FORMATTING THE OUTPUT

Once you select the location for your output, you must specify what the content of the output will be. You can output values of the variables in your data step, and you can output any labels and messages that you wish. As with inputting, you output one line at a time, specifying characters and spaces from left to right.

The specification of output is done with a PUT statement. The PUT statement is like an INPUT statement in that it lists variables to be output and their format. If you wish to read a file and copy it to another, identical file, you might use the same format specification on the INPUT and PUT statement. The PUT statement has an additional feature, however, and that is the addition of comments to be output. These comments, which can serve as labels or messages, are placed in single or double quotation marks to distinguish them from variable names or column designations.

For example, suppose as in Program 1.1 that your data step calculated the mean of several scores. The variable containing the mean might be called MEANX. You could output MEANX with the simple statement

```
PUT MEANX;
```

Outputting will be done using the default format and output for MEANX. If, however, you wish to control the location on the data line where the variable is placed, you would enter a designation, such as

```
PUT MEANX 5-10;
```

This statement will put MEANX in columns 5 to 10.

Finally, you may wish to label the output. A statement such as

```
PUT 'MEANX = ' MEANX;
```

will produce output that looks like

```
MEANX = 34.8
```

PROC PRINT

PROC PRINT is a feature that causes the contents of a SAS data set to be output to the output window. The output of a PROC PRINT contains not only the data for each case but also the variable names. This format, with each variable labeled, makes PROC PRINT a valuable tool when you wish to examine variable values for individual cases, or when you want to see which variables are in a file. PROC PRINT can be run by inserting the statement

```
PROC PRINT;
```

in the appropriate place in your program. Its proper location is at the end of a data step. As with all PROCs, PROC PRINT cannot come in the middle of a data step, because it ends processing of the statements for a data step. Unless otherwise specified, PROC PRINT prints the contents of the most recent data step that preceded it. If there were several data steps, the closest one would be outputted. An earlier data set can be specified with the DATA= option, as in

```
PROC PRINT DATA=FIRST;
```

or

```
PROC PRINT DATA=SURVEY3;
```

Output 2.1 contains two examples of PROC PRINT. As can be seen, each PROC PRINT table contains the variable names as headers for each column. The first column, labeled "OBS," contains the number of the case, from 1 to the number of cases. The remaining columns contain the values for each variable.

There are several options and optional statements associated with PROC PRINT. For example, the VAR statement allows you to specify that only certain variables will be printed. Thus, you might wish to examine only a subset of the variables in the data set. For example,

```
PROC PRINT; VAR POP GNP;
```

would output only the variables POP and GNP. Additional options allow you to modify the format of the PROC PRINT output. Details can be found in the SAS documentation.

EXAMPLE OF INPUTTING
AND OUTPUTTING

Suppose you have data from a study of statewide violent crime as a function of economic conditions and education quality. For the sake of this example, data were generated (made up) from six states on three variables—the violent crime rate (number of crimes per 10,000 residents), the unemployment rate, and the statewide expenditure per student in the public schools.

The purpose of Program 2.1 is to input the data from a file on disk and output it in a format that would be easy to read. This is done both with a PUT statement and with a PROC PRINT. As an additional purpose, Program 2.1 creates a SAS data set that duplicates each case. This example illustrates the function of the OUTPUT statement.

The steps involved in accomplishing Program 2.1's tasks are listed in Table 2.3. These steps could have been placed in a flowchart, but considering the simplicity of the program, the list of steps is certainly sufficient for preplanning the program. As can be seen, the program has two data steps (Steps 1 and 5 in the table). The first data step inputs data from an external file (Step 2). The contents of the data set are outputted using two procedures (Steps 3 and 4).

Output 2.1

Output From FILE PRINT

The SAS System

```
Crime = 230  Unemployment = 8.2  State per pupil expenditure = $2100
Crime = 250  Unemployment = 7.3  State per pupil expenditure = $2750
Crime = 350  Unemployment = 9.1  State per pupil expenditure = $1750
Crime = 150  Unemployment = 6.5  State per pupil expenditure = $2250
Crime = 100  Unemployment = 4.9  State per pupil expenditure = $3100
Crime = 200  Unemployment = 7.7  State per pupil expenditure = $2600
```

Output From PROC PRINT for First Data Step

The SAS System

```
OBS   CRIMERAT   UNEMP   EDUC
 1      230       8.2    2100
 2      250       7.3    2750
 3      350       9.1    1750
 4      150       6.5    2250
 5      100       4.9    3100
 6      200       7.7    2600
```

Output From PROC PRINT for Second Data Step

The SAS System

```
OBS   CRIMERAT   UNEMP   EDUC
 1      230       8.2    2100
 2      230       8.2    2100
 3      250       7.3    2750
 4      250       7.3    2750
 5      350       9.1    1750
 6      350       9.1    1750
 7      150       6.5    2250
 8      150       6.5    2250
 9      100       4.9    3100
10      100       4.9    3100
11      200       7.7    2600
12      200       7.7    2600
```

The second data step (Step 5) inputs data from the SAS data set created in the prior data step (Step 6). It outputs twice to the SAS data set (Step 7) and outputs the contents with PROC PRINT (Step 8).

The listing of the SAS statements is in Program 2.1. Comments were placed before each of the two DATA statements to describe briefly what each data

---

Table 2.3
Step-by-Step Procedure for Program 2.1

1. Begin a data step.
2. Input data from the file A:CRIME.DAT.
3. Output the data to FILE PRINT
4. PROC PRINT the contents of the SAS data set.
5. Create a new data step.
6. Input data from prior SAS data set.
7. Output each case twice to SAS data set.
8. PROC PRINT the current SAS data set.

---

step was designed to accomplish. Notice that the comments begin with an asterisk and end with a semicolon. Both comments are spread over two lines. The asterisk is found only at the beginning of the first line, and the semicolon is found only at the end of the final line of a comment. Each line of the program is numbered only for illustrative purposes. Line numbers should not be placed in a SAS program.

The first data step begins with line 3, which creates the SAS data set, named CRIME. The INFILE statement (line 4) says to input this file, which is located on a diskette in floppy drive A on a PC. It could be located in a different floppy drive, on a hard disk, or on some other storage device. The INPUT statement (line 5) reads three variables: CRIMERAT, UNEMP, and EDUC. Note that the number of columns for each variable is specified. CRIMERAT occupies the first three columns, UNEMP is in the next two columns, and EDUC is in the next four columns for each case.

Line 6 directs the output to the output window. The *PUT* statement (lines 7-9) indicates what and how to output. This particular statement says to

1. Print " Crime = " (Note the blank space after the equal sign),

2. Print the value of

3. Skip to column 15,

4. Print "

5. Print the value of UNEMP for this case,

6. Skip to column 35,

7. Print " Education = " (Note no blank space after the dollar sign), and

8. Print the value of

The PUT statement will be performed for each case in the data set. In this example, it will be executed six times. The top of Output 2.1 shows the output from this data step using the PUT statement. As you can see, there are six lines, which are the same except for the values of the variables.

Line 10 of Program 2.1 contains the statement PROC PRINT, which is all that is necessary to output the entire contents of the SAS data set CRIME. The middle of Output 2.1 shows the results of the PROC PRINT. As with the PUT statement, the PROC PRINT generates six lines of data. The format of the output is somewhat different. The names of the variables are printed only once each as column headers, and the observation numbers are shown.

Line 12 of Program 2.1 begins another data step. This time the SAS data set is named TWO. Data are input to this data set from the SAS data set CRIME that was created by the prior data step. Because the program has continued to execute, the temporary SAS data set can be used. Line 13 uses a SET statement to input the data.

Lines 14 and 15 contain OUTPUT statements. Each one causes the currently processed case to be output to the SAS data set named TWO. Thus, each case will be output twice, and the resulting SAS data set will have duplicate lines. Line 16 is a PROC PRINT statement, which accomplishes the outputting of the current data set named TWO.

The bottom of Output 2.1 shows the results of the PROC PRINT. As can be seen, there are 12 lines, representing 12 cases. Each pair of cases has identical values for the three variables.

WRITING REPORTS WITH PUT STATEMENTS

PUT statements can be used to write reports combining messages with data. Generally these reports are output to the output window or to a file on a diskette, on a hard drive, or on another storage device. Tables can be produced that may be immediately usable for many situations, such as reports or articles. This eliminates the extra work of taking the data from the output window and manually inserting them into a table with a word processor. The ability to set up a report can be particularly useful for routine reports where the format remains constant but the data change from time to time.

Writing reports involves an extension of the procedures discussed above. You specify the contents of each line of the report. A report might begin with a title or brief description. Often columns and/or rows are labeled. Comments and notes can be placed at the bottom. You can also produce a narrative report, inserting values of variables where appropriate. Although the SAS PUT statement is useful for reports, it is somewhat cumbersome if you wish to produce a long, narrative document.

Program 2.2 shows a SAS program and Output 2.2 shows the resulting report that it generated. The program contains two features that have not yet been covered. The first is the automatic case number indicator _N_. As cases are input from a file, the SAS System numbers them consecutively, beginning at 1. It creates a variable _N_ that contains the case number for each case. The first case will have a value of 1 for _N_, the second case will have a value of 2, and so on. You can refer to a particular case by its number. One use for this is to do something only for the first case, as has been done here.

The second new feature is the IF statement. The statement

```
IF _N_ = 1 THEN . . .
```

says to do what comes after the THEN only for case 1. With the current example, this results in printing the title information only once, for the first case. It also results in the printing of the note at the bottom of the report only for the last case. These logical statements will be covered in greater detail in Chapter 4.

This program inputs for each case an identification number and a social security number. It then creates two reports. The first is a listing of the social security numbers for each case. The second is a listing of the identification numbers only.

Data step REPORT inputs two variables, ID and SSN (see line 2) from the CARDS portion of the program. It then writes the report shown in Output 2.2. The third line directs output to print to the output window. The fourth and fifth lines of the program say to output a message only for the first case. Beginning at column 10, the message "Listing of Social Security Numbers" is printed. The

Program 2.2
Example of a SAS Generated Report Using Put Statements

```
 1    DATA REPORT
 2    INPUT ID 1-2 SSN 3-11;
 3    FILE PRINT;
 4  IF _N_ = 1 THEN PUT @10 'Listing of
Social Security
 5       Numbers'/;
 6    PUT @5 'Case #' ID '= ' SSN;
 7    IF _N_ = 5 THEN PUT /@10 'This
Concludes The Report.';
 8  DATALINES;
 9  01237827122
10 02873542348
11 11912612738
12 15231623067
13 23332528907
14 ;
15 DATA REPORT2;
16    SET REPORT;
17    FILE PRINT;
18    PUT +5 'ID = ' ID @;
19 RUN;
```

"/" says to skip a line. The sixth line says to print the data for a case. As you can see from the output, each line is the same, except for the case number and actual variable value. Because there is no IF statement to restrict the output, a line will be produced for each case in the file. Each time the PUT statement is executed, a new line is output. Line 7 says that for the fifth case, a line should be skipped and the message "This Concludes The Report" should be printed. The message begins in column 10.

Data step REPORT2 (line 15) illustrates the use of the trailing @ on a PUT statement (line 18). Without the trailing @, a new line will begin each time the PUT is executed. The trailing @ says to keep track of the current line and column and to resume printing at that point when the next PUT statement is encountered. The PUT statement in this data step says to

Output 2.2
Output From Data Set REPORT

```
The SAS System

      Listing of Social Security Numbers

Case #1 = 237827122
Case #2 = 873542348
Case #11 = 912612738
Case #15 = 231623067
Case #23 = 332528907


         This Concludes The Report.

     Output From Data Set REPORT2

The SAS System

ID = 1   ID = 2   ID = 11   ID = 15   ID = 23
```

1. Skip 5 spaces,

2. Print " ID = ",

3. Print the value of ID, and

4. Hold the present print position.

The results can be seen in Output 2.2. The five output blocks are strung out on a single line with several spaces between them. If the end of the line on the screen or printer had been encountered, output would have continued on the following line. Although it may not be apparent from this example why you would want to print on a single line, there may be times when you want to print something from one case and then wait until the processing of a subsequent case before printing the remainder of a line.

USING PROC PRINT AND PUT FOR DEBUGGING

To check for logical errors in your program, you must check that all variables were properly input and that all computations produced the intended results. The PROC PRINT can be useful in showing the values of all variables input as well as the final values of all variables manipulated. The PUT command used in conjunction with a FILE PRINT allows greater control in allowing values of variables to be output at various stages in the program. In other words, you decide which variables are output and at which point in the program. This is not an issue with the simple programs in this chapter, but it will become increasingly important as our programs become more and more complex.

Once all syntax errors have been fixed, you should immediately run your program with a PROC PRINT following the data step. This will produce a listing of all data for each case. Be sure to check the input data against the corresponding values in the PROC PRINT. It is quite easy to make a mistake on an INPUT statement and read the wrong columns. This will result in mislabeling of the variables (e.g., the income variable really indicates religion), reading in the wrong numbers (e.g., a two-digit number being read as one digit), or in missing values if blank columns are read by mistake. Be sure to check more than just the first or last case. Sometimes the first case or few cases are read correctly, and an error occurs later. It is best to check the first case, the last case, and a few at random in the middle of the file to be sure everything read properly. Keep in mind that if your program changed values of the variable, the PROC PRINT will show the final value and not the value originally read.

If a data set is large, it is a good idea to limit the number of cases to be retained in with an IF statement, as in

```
IF _N_ < 11;
```

which will send only the first 10 cases to PROC PRINT.

The PROC PRINT will also output all variables created within the data step. The programs in this chapter did not create new variables, but programs in subsequent chapters will do this.

When using a PUT statement, it is a good idea to include a comment so that you can easily tell where each printed value came from, as in

```
PUT 'Output from line 20, X = ' X;
```

This will print a message that the value of X outputted came from line 20.

COMMON ERRORS

Although the programs in this chapter were quite simple, it is still easy to make logical errors. With inputting, the most common errors involve misreading data (i.e., reading the wrong columns or the wrong variables). As noted in the prior section, you can use a PROC PRINT to check that the variables are read properly. One thing to be particularly careful about is reading data beyond the current line. As noted in the section "Inputting Data Lines," the MISSOVER can be used to help prevent SAS from reading onto the following line if there are missing data at the end of a line. Look for a warning that SAS read beyond the current line to indicate this problem.

When a case has data on more than one line, there is potential for errors if there are missing lines in your data file. SAS will not know that the line is missing, and it will skip to the next line in the data set, even though it isn't the right one. Thus, with two lines per case, if case 40 is missing the second line, the program will assume the first line for case 41 is the missing line. All subsequent cases will be mixed up and read incorrectly. A warning to look for is that there was a "Lost Card." This says that the number of data lines was not evenly divisible by the number of lines indicated per case on the **INPUT** statement.

For outputting, similar errors can occur. You must be careful to specify the proper variables to output and to have them in the correct position in your report. A common error is to indicate the wrong variable name. The report may look correct, but the numbers output are wrong. This must be checked by running a test problem to see if the report is correct.

～ *Debugging Exercises* ～

Each of the following programs contains one or more errors. The best way to do this exercise is to enter it into your SAS editor, run it, and then proceed to fix the errors, rerunning until you are satisfied the programs are correct. A list of corrections can be found in Appendix E.

Exercise 2.1

```
data a;
input a b c d
datalines;
1 2 3 4
5 6 7 8
;
total = a + b + c + d;
proc print;
run;
```

Exercise 2.2

```
data employment;
input state 1-10 civilianworkforce 6.1
unemployfeb2000 2.1 unemployjuly2000 2.1;
change = unemployjuly2000 - unemployfeb2000;
file print;
put "Table of Unemployment Rates By State"/;
put "State" "Change in Unemployment Rate";
put state @25 change;
datalines;
alabama 218964641
alaska 31885855
arizona 239223936
arkansas 126224741
california 1695124650
;
run;
```

Chapter 3

Programming Algebraic and Mathematical Operations

Chapter 2 covered the inputting and outputting of data from within the SAS data step. There are instances when this is all you wish to do. For example, you might wish to combine two or more files, then output the contents to a new file. Most of the time, however, your program is intended to manipulate the data within the data step. You might wish to combine variables, transform variables, create new variables as functions of old variables, and delete variables or cases. Examples of manipulations include the following: summing items of a psychological test to yield subscale scores, transforming observations (e.g., square or log) so that they more closely meet the assumptions for analysis of variance or to test for curvilinear relations, and combining monthly productivity data to yield an annual total or average.

The techniques covered in this chapter will allow you to perform these sorts of algebraic and mathematical manipulations of your data. This chapter will focus on operations that are done within each case individually. The following chapter will explore procedures for doing calculations involving multiple cases.

ARITHMETIC OPERATORS

Arithmetic operators specify the arithmetic operations of addition, subtraction, multiplication, division, and raising to a power (e.g., squaring). The operators are shown in Table 3.1, along with their order of priority, which will be discussed later.

These operators are used with SAS expressions. An expression is a statement that defines the value of a variable. It begins with a variable name followed by an equal sign ("="). To the right of the equal sign is the value or function that you wish to define the variable as. You can define an existing variable to be equal to something, or you can define a new variable to be equal to something.

The simplest expression is one that defines a variable to be equal to a constant. Examples would be

```
X = 15;
Y = -37;
Income = 31200;
```

The first expression defines the variable X to have the numeric value of 15, the second defines Y as having the value of -37, and the third defines Income to be equal to 31200. You can also define character variables to have character strings as their values, as in

```
Location = 'Washington, D.C.';
```

Note that the character string is in quotes (single or double are interchangeable).

You can use expressions to define a variable as a function of another variable, as in

Table 3.1		
SAS® Language Arithmetic Operators		
Operator	Function	Priority
**	Raise to a Power	1
*	Multiplication	2
/	Division	2
+	Addition	3
−	Subtraction	3

```
Y = 3 * X;
MoIncome = Income / 12;
XSquared = X ** 2;
Diff = A - B;
```

In the first example, Y is defined to be equal to 3 times X, in the second MoIncome is Income divided by 12, in the third XSquared is X squared, and in the fourth, Diff is A minus B. The spacing within each expression is for readability and is unnecessary. For example, the first expression could have been

```
Y=3*X;
```

Expressions can be complex, involving several variables and several operations. One thing to keep in mind with complex expressions is the order in which operations are carried out. For example, the answer to the operation

```
Y = 3 * 4 + 5
```

depends on whether you do the multiplication or addition first. If you multiply 3 * 4 first, then add 5 to the result, you will get Y = 17. If you add 4 + 5 and then multiply by 3, you will get Y = 27.

Operators are executed within an expression in **priority** order. As shown in Table 3.1, raising to a power is first priority, multiplication and division are second priority, and addition and subtraction are third priority. With an expression such as the one above, the multiplication will be done before the addition because its priority is higher. If this is the order desired, then

```
Y = 3 * 4 + 5
```

could be entered. If you wish to do the addition first, then you must use parentheses, as you would in algebra, to override the priority order, as in

```
Y = 3 * (4 + 5)
```

With complex expressions, it can be easier to read, and debug, if you make liberal use of parentheses, even when not needed, as in

```
Y = ((A + B + C)/(A * B)) - (X**2*(A - B)/C);
```

Note that there are double parentheses used in two places. This is necessary to avoid ambiguity about which operations are to be done first. The parts of the expression in the innermost parentheses are executed before the parts in the outermost parentheses. Thus, the sum of (A + B + C) and the product of A * B will be done before the former term is divided by the latter. There must be an equal number of left and right parentheses in every expression; otherwise, your SAS Log will contain an error message that the parentheses don't balance. Note also that not all of the parentheses are necessary. The ones that are underlined are unnecessary, but they make it easier to trace through what the expression is supposed to do.

Addition and subtraction can be done in any order, so if your expression involves only these two operations, parentheses are unnecessary. Likewise, multiplication and division can be done in any order. It is only when you mix priority order operators that the order becomes critical. A very frequent error with such expressions is to forget to use parentheses, so that the computations are done in the wrong order.

SAS FUNCTIONS

A **function** is like a built-in expression that allows you to define a variable as being equal to a specified mathematical quantity. For example,

```
Y = SQRT(X);
```

defines Y as being equal to the square root of X. Every function, like an expression, begins with a variable name followed by an equal sign. To the right is the function name and one or more **arguments** listed in parentheses. These arguments can be a number or the name of a variable. In the above example, X is the argument to the square root function. The statement

```
Y = SQRT(16);
```

is also valid. It will set Y equal to 4.

One of the valuable features of the SAS language is the inclusion of an extensive list of functions. Release 6.11 of the SAS language has almost 150 different functions, and Release 8.01 has more than 200. These include not only mathematical functions (algebraic, econometric, trigonomic, and statistical) but also various date and ZIP code functions. Date functions allow you to calculate the number of days between calendar dates. ZIP code functions give you or return the state name from the ZIP code that you enter. Thus, if your argument is 33620, the function will tell you that the ZIP code is in Florida.

Although an extensive treatment of the various functions would be beyond the scope of this book, Table 3.2 contains the name, format, and purpose of the functions most likely to be used for statistical data analysis. Each is briefly discussed below. The SAS documentation should be consulted for the details on the other SAS functions.

ABS

The ABS function gives you or returns the absolute value of the argument. For example,

Table 3.2
Selected SAS® Language Functions

Function	Syntax	Purpose
ABS	Y = ABS(X)	Absolute value of X
COMB[a]	Y = COMB(n, r)	Number of combinations of n elements r at a time
COS	Y = COS(X)	Cosine of X where X is in radians
CSS	Y = CSS(. . .)	Corrected sum of squares of arguments
EXP	Y = EXP(X)	e to the X power
FACT[a]	Y = FACT(X)	Factorial of X
INT	Y = INT(X)	Rounds X to its whole number
KURTOSIS	Y = KURTOSIS(. . .)	Kurtosis of argument values
LOG	Y = LOG(X)	Natural log (Base e) of X
LOG10	Y = LOG10(X)	Common log (Base 10) of X
MEAN	Y = MEAN(. . .)	Mean of argument values
MOD	Y = MOD(A,B)	Remainder of A divided by B
PERM[a]	Y = PERM(n,r)	Number of permutations of n elements r at a time
PROBCHI	Y = PROBCHI(C,DF)	Probability of chi square value C with DF degrees of freedom
PROBF	Y = PROBF(F,DN,DD)	Probability of F value F with degrees of freedom = DN for numerator and DD for denominator
PROBNORM	Y = PROBNORM(Z)	Probability for normal distribution where Z is the standard score
PROBT	Y = PROBT(T,DF)	Probability of t value T with DF degrees of freedom
RANNOR	Y = RANNOR(seed)	Generates random numbers from a normal distribution
RANUNI	Y = RANUNI(seed)	Generates random numbers from a uniform distribution
ROUND	Y = ROUND(X)	Rounds X to its nearest integer
SIN	Y = SIN(X)	Sine of X where X is in radians
SKEWNESS	Y = SKEWNESS(. . .)	Skewness of arguments
SQRT	Y = SQRT(X)	Square root of X
STD	Y = STD(. . .)	Standard deviation estimate of arguments
STDERR	Y = STDERR(. . .)	Standard error of mean of arguments
SUM	Y = SUM(...)	Sum of arguments
TAN	Y = TAN(X)	Tangent of X where X is in radians
USS	Y = USS(...)	Uncorrected sum of squares of arguments
VAR	Y = VAR(...)	Variance estimate of arguments

NOTE: a. Not available in Release 6.

```
Y = ABS(6);
```

and

```
Y = ABS(-6);
```

return a Y value of 6.

Descriptive Statistics Functions

Several functions are available to return descriptive statistics on the list of arguments provided. In other words, you enter the list of numbers for which you wish to calculate the descriptive statistics. You can also calculate the statistical function of interest across a series of variables within each case, which is a more frequent use of these functions. To accomplish this, you must add the "OF" statement to the argument list, as in

```
GPA = MEAN(OF GRADE1-GRADE10);
```

This statement will calculate the mean of variables listed as arguments—in this case GRADE1 to GRADE10. This presumes that you have 10 variables named GRADE numbered consecutively from 1 to 10. You can also list individual variables, as in

```
WEEKLY = MEAN(OF MON,TUES,WED,THUR,FRI,SAT,SUN);
```

SUM calculates the sum of the arguments. USS calculates the sum of the arguments squared, or

$$Y = \Sigma X^2.$$

CSS calculates the corrected sum of squares, adjusting each observation for the mean using the formula

$$Y = \Sigma(X - M)^2,$$

where M is the mean of the X values.

```
Y = SUM(1,2,3)
```

will return a value of 6 (1 + 2 + 3).

```
Y = USS(1,2,3)
```

will return a value of 14 (1 + 4 + 9).

```
Y = CSS(1,2,3)
```

will return a value of 2 (1 + 0 + 1).

STD will give you the standard deviation of the arguments, and VAR will give you the variance. In both cases, the formula is for the unbiased estimate, where the corrected sum of squares is divided by the sample size minus one. STDERR gives you the standard error of the mean, where the variance estimate is divided by the sample size, and the square root of the resultant is calculated. Thus,

```
STD(1,2,3,4,5)
```

will return a value of 1.58114,

```
VAR(1,2,3,4,5)
```

will return a value of 2.5, and

```
STDERR(1,2,3,4,5)
```

will return a value of .70711.

SKEWNESS returns the skewness of the arguments. KURTOSIS returns the kurtosis of the arguments.

When variable names are specified as arguments, all these functions will ignore missing values. For example, suppose you wish to compute the sum of five items (ITEM1 to ITEM5) from a psychological test. The functions will return the sum of the existing values when there are missing values. Thus, the sums for different cases may be based on different numbers of variables. You must be careful with missing data that you do not misinterpret the scores of cases that had missing values. By contrast, if you compute the sum with an expression, as in

```
TOTAL = ITEM1 + ITEM2 + ITEM3 + ITEM4 + ITEM5;
```

TOTAL will be assigned a missing value for any case that has one or more missing items.

Log and Exponential Functions

LOG gives you the natural log, which is the log to the base e (e = 2.71828), whereas LOG10 gives you the common log, which is the log to the base 10. LOG(10) will return the value of 2.302585093. LOG10(10) will return the value of 1. You will get an error if you try to take the log of a negative number.

EXP gives you the number produced by raising the constant e to the power specified by the argument. Thus, EXP(1) = 2.71828, while EXP(0) = 1.

MOD

MOD returns the remainder of a division operation. For example, Y = MOD(5,3) will return 2 because 5 divided by 3 leaves 2 as the remainder.

Factorials, Combinations, and Permutations (Release 8)

FACT provides the factorial of the argument provided (i.e., the product of the integers from 1 to the argument). For example, Y = FACT(5) will return 120 (1 × 2 × 3 × 4 × 5).

COMB gives the combinations of *n* things taken *r* at a time, with *n* as the first and *r* as the second argument. For example, Y = COMB(4, 2) will return 6. PERM gives the permutations of *n* things taken *r* at a time. For example, Y = PERM(4, 2) will return 12.

Probability Distributions

The SAS language has several probability distribution functions. Four distributions will be discussed here—normal, t, F, and chi square. With these functions, you enter the value of a statistic and the appropriate degrees of freedom. The function returns the exact probability of finding a value less than the one entered.

PROBNORM gives you the probability of finding a standard score that is less than the argument score on the normal distribution. You enter the score, and the function gives you the probability. The statement $Y = PROBNORM(1.96)$ will return the value .975. This is because the probability of finding a value of 1.96 or less on the normal distribution is .975.

PROBT gives you the probability of finding a t value less than the one you enter as the first argument, given the degrees of freedom entered as the second argument. The statement $Y = PROBT(2,100)$ will return the value of .97589.

PROBF gives you the probability of finding an F value less than the one you enter as the first argument, given the numerator and denominator degrees of freedom entered as the second and third arguments, respectively. The statement $Y = PROBF(4,1,100)$ will return a value of .95179.

PROBCHI gives you the probability of finding a chi square value less than the one you enter as the first argument, given the degrees of freedom as the second argument. The statement $Y = PROBCHI(4,2)$ will return a value of .86466.

Random Number Generators

The SAS language has several random number generators. Perhaps the most useful are the uniform and normal generators, RANUNI and RANNOR, respectively. Both generators need a starting value or **seed** from which the random numbers are generated. A negative value for the seed will tell the computer to use the time value from its internal clock as the seed. Thus, each time you run the SAS program the seed, and thus the set of random numbers, will be different. A positive value for a seed will be the actual seed used. This is useful if you wish to use the same set of random numbers each time, which you might wish to do when testing and debugging your program.

RANUNI generates numbers from a uniform distribution with values from 0 to 1. This distribution is one in which every possible value has an equal theoretical frequency. The range of values can be changed with a mathematical operation. To increase the range of possible values, multiply by the range desired, as in

```
Y = 10 * RANUNI(-4);
```

This statement will generate a uniform number from a distribution with a range from 0 to 10. It uses the computer's clock to generate its seed. If you wish to keep the minimum value at 0, just multiply by the maximum value desired; however, if you wish to change the location of the range of numbers, for example to begin at 1 or to include negative numbers, you must add the minimum value desired. To make the minimum value a +1, add 1 to the number generated, as in

```
Y = 1 + RANUNI(-4);
```

To make the distribution range from −1 to +1, you must increase its range to 2 by multiplying by 2, then add −1 to the result to make the minimum value equal to −1, as in

```
Y = -1 + 2 * RANUNI(-2);
```

RANNOR returns numbers from a normal distribution with a mean of 0 and a variance of 1. The mean and standard deviation can be modified by multiplying the function by the desired standard deviation and adding the desired mean. To generate numbers from a distribution with a mean of 100 and a standard deviation of 10, use the following function:

```
Y = 100 + 10*RANNOR(-2);
```

Rounding Functions

There are two rounding functions, INT and ROUND. INT truncates numbers by dropping whatever part of the number is to the right of the decimal point. ROUND rounds numbers to their nearest specified unit. Unless otherwise indicated, numbers are rounded to their nearest integer. INT(3.1), INT(3.5), and INT(3.9) all equal 3. ROUND(3.1) equals 3, but ROUND(3.5) and ROUND(3.9) both equal 4.

With the ROUND function, you can specify the units to which you wish to round with the second argument. If you wish to round to the nearest integer, enter 1 as the second argument. If you wish to round to the nearest 10th, enter .1. For example,

```
Y = ROUND(123.456,1)
```

will return 123,

```
Y = ROUND(123.456,.1)
```

will return 123.5,

```
Y = ROUND(123.456,.01)
```

will return 123.46, and

```
Y = ROUND(123.456,100)
```

will return 100.

SQRT

As noted earlier, SQRT gives you the square root of the argument.

Trigonomic Functions

The COS, SIN, and TAN functions return the cosine, sine, and tangent of their arguments, respectively. The argument must be in radians. For example,

```
A = COS(.785398163)
```

will return a cosine of .7071,

```
B = SIN(.785398163)
```

will return a sine of .7071, and

```
C = TAN(.785398163)
```

will return a tangent of 1.0. (Note that .785398163 in radians equals 45 degrees.)

DELETING VARIABLES
FROM A SAS DATA SET

There are times when you may wish to delete variables from the SAS data set that is being built by the current data step. This frequently occurs when you combine individual observations into aggregate scores, then analyze only the aggregate scores. For example, with psychological tests, you might combine individual items into total scale scores and analyze only the totals.

You have two options for deleting variables within a data step. You can specify the variables to delete from the data set with the DROP statement. Alternately, you can specify the variables you don't wish to delete with a KEEP statement. To avoid confusion and possible conflicts, you should use only one of these two types of statements within a given SAS data step.

Both statements have the same syntax. You give the statement name DROP or KEEP, followed by a list of variables you wish to drop or keep. Variables that are numbered in a range (e.g., X1 to X50), can be referred to as

```
DROP X1-X50;
```

Variables with different alphabetical character names can be listed by name. They can also be listed in order using two dashes ("– –") as in

```
KEEP A--Z;
```

The SAS System keeps track of the order in which it encounters variables within a data step. The variables entered on an INPUT statement are kept in the same order as they were listed in that statement. Variables created with expressions are kept in the order in which the expression statements are listed. To include a range of variables, the SAS System will use the data step's order of variables to decide which ones fall within the range specified. The statement

```
KEEP A--D;
```

will include the variables A, B, C, and D, if the data step used the INPUT statement

```
INPUT A B C D;
```

It will include only the variables A and D if the data step used the INPUT statement

```
INPUT A D C B;
```

When in doubt about the order of variables, use PROC PRINT to output variables in the SAS data set's order. Unless the SAS data set contains very few cases, it is a good idea to limit the file size to a few cases with an IF . . . statement. For example, to limit the output to two cases, insert the following statement in the data step before the PROC PRINT:

```
IF _N_ < 3;
```

The use of the IF statement will be discussed in Chapter 4.

If you use a DROP or KEEP within a data step, the deleted variables are still available for processing within the data step. If you save the data step to a SAS data library, however, or if you access the data step's data set from another data step, the deleted variables will be gone. Any PROCs run on the data step will not be able to access the deleted variables, and if you try you will get an error that the variable is uninitialized, which means it doesn't exist.

EXAMPLES USING FUNCTIONS

A common task in many studies is to compute descriptive statistics across several variables for each case. This can happen when subjects complete multiple-item tests or questionnaires. Functions can be used to compute sums

Program 3.1
Using Functions to Compute Descriptive Statistics

```
1DATA SUMMARY;
 2 INPUT ITEM1-ITEM10;
 3 ISUM = SUM(OF ITEM1-ITEM10);
 4 IMEAN = MEAN(OF ITEM1-ITEM10);
 5 ISS = CSS(OF ITEM1-ITEM10);
 6 ISD = STD(OF ITEM1-ITEM10);
 7 IVAR = VAR(OF ITEM1-ITEM10);
 8 ISD = ROUND(ISD,.01);
 9 IVAR = ROUND(IVAR,.01);
10 FILE PRINT;
11 IF _N_ = 1 THEN PUT
12  @20 'Descriptive Statistics for Items 1 to
10'/;
13 IF _N_ = 1 THEN PUT @3 'Sum' @15 'Mean' @27
14  'Sum of Squares' @46 'SD' @62 'VAR' /;
15 PUT @4 ISUM @16 IMEAN @31 ISS @46 ISD @61 IVAR;
16 DATALINES;
17 2 3 2 5 7 1 8 5 9 5
18 ;
19 RUN;
```

and means, as well as more complex descriptive statistics. Program 3.1 illustrates the use of SAS functions to generate descriptive statistics for 10 variables, named ITEM1 to ITEM10. The sum, mean, sum of squares, standard deviation, and variance are computed. Table 3.3 is a step-by-step specification of what the program does. The program starts by beginning a data step (Step 1). It then inputs the data for the 10 variables (Step 2) and computes the descriptive statistics (Step 3). Two of the summary statistics need to be rounded (Step 4). Finally, a report is generated with the results (Step 5).

The SAS statements can be seen in Program 3.1. By now much of this program should look familiar. The SAS data set is called SUMMARY (see line 1). The input statement (line 2) uses list input to enter the 10 variables, ITEM1 to ITEM10. Functions are used in the following five statements (lines 3 to 7) to calculate the descriptive statistics wanted. The ROUND function is used to round the standard deviation (line 8) and variance (line 9) to two digits to the right of

---

Table 3.3
Step-by-Step Procedure for Program 3.1

1. Begin a data step
2. Input 10 variables
3. Compute descriptive statistics with functions
4. Round the standard deviation and variance with a ROUND function
5. Output the results

---

the decimal. The remainder of the data step generates the report in Output 3.1 using features discussed in Chapter 2.

Program 3.2 illustrates the use of the probability functions to determine the exact significance level for the *t*, chi square, *F*, and normal distributions. There may be times when a researcher wishes to know the exact probability for a given test statistic, and these values cannot be found in tables, except for the *z* test. In Program 3.2, there are no data inputted from outside the data step; rather, the data that are manipulated are defined as constants (see lines 2 to 4) or are entered directly into the function, as with line 8, where a value of 3.12 was placed in the function.

This program first defines the values of the *t*, chi square, and *F* statistics, as well as their degrees of freedom as constants (lines 2 to 4). Functions are then used to compute the appropriate probabilities (lines 5 to 7). Because the functions return the proportion of the distribution that falls to the left of the

Output 3.1

```
The SAS System

Descriptive Statistics for Items 1 to 10

Sum    Mean  Sum of Squares SD        VAR

47     4.7   66.1     2.71          7.34
```

Program 3.2
Program to Compute Exact Probabilities of Statistical Tests

```
1   DATA SIGNIF;
2    T = 3.37; DFT = 28;
3    CHI = 6.34; DFCHI = 3;
4    F = 8.91; DFN = 3; DFD = 42;
5    TPROB = 1 - PROBT(T,DFT);
6    CHIPROB = 1 - PROBCHI(CHI,DFCHI);
7    FPROB = 1 - PROBF(F,DFN,DFD);
8    NORMPROB= ROUND(1 - PROBNORM(3.12),.0001);
9    TPROB = ROUND(TPROB,.0001);
10   CHIPROB = ROUND(CHIPROB,.0001);
11   FPROB = ROUND(FPROB,.0001);
12   FILE PRINT;
13   PUT 'Probability For T With ' DFT 'Degrees Of
     Freedom = 'TPROB;
     PUT / 'Probability For Chi Square With ' DFCHI
        'Degrees Of Freedom = ' CHIPROB;
     PUT / 'Probability For F With ' DFN 'And ' DFD
        'Degrees of Freedom = ' FPROB;
     PUT / 'Probability For Z = ' NORMPROB;
     RUN;
```

entered value, each is subtracted from 1 to yield the significance level. Each of these tests is one-tailed and gives the probability for the uppermost tail of the distribution. This is typically what you want for chi square and F tests. For t and the normal distribution, you should enter the absolute value if the statistic has a negative sign. If you wish two-tailed tests for t and the normal distribution, the probabilities generated should be doubled. You might attempt this modification as an exercise. Hint: Just multiply TPROB and NORMPROB by 2.

Note that one function was embedded inside of another in the statement in line 8. Functions can be nested in one another, with the results of one function serving as the argument to another. In this case first the *PROBNORM* function is computed, and then the result is rounded to the nearest 10,000th. The other probabilities were rounded with separate ROUND functions (lines 9 to 11).

Output 3.2

```
The SAS System
Probability For T With 28 Degrees Of Freedom = 0.0011
Probability For Chi Square With 3 Degrees Of Freedom = 0.0962
Probability For F With 3 And 42 Degrees Of Freedom = 0.0001
Probability For Z = 0.0009
```

Lines 12 to 18 produce the report shown in Output 3.2. There are no new features in these statements, but they illustrate how you can insert the values of variables into message statements in reports.

This program could have been written to input the appropriate data from an external file. If this were a program you were going to run on several values of the statistics, it would be easier to set it up this way. To look up an occasional value, the approach used in this example program works quite well.

COMMON ERRORS

The most common error with complex expressions involves mistakes with parentheses. As noted in this chapter, there is a priority order with operators, and often parentheses are required to force operations in the intended order. Parentheses must be used in pairs, and if a pair is unbalanced (e.g., there are five left and only four right parentheses), you will get a syntax error. Improper use of parentheses can also cause logical errors if operations are done in an incorrect order. Be sure to run some tests on complex expressions, perhaps by placing a PUT statement immediately after the statement, to be sure it works correctly.

Another potential problem is confusion between the INT and ROUND expressions. Be sure you use INT when you want to truncate to the right of the decimal and ROUND if you want to round to the nearest whole number. Also be aware that using the probability functions can be tricky, so be sure you have adjusted for two-tailed tests if that is what's intended, and be sure you are indicating the intended tail of the distribution.

∾ *Debugging Exercises* ∾

Exercise 3.1

```
data functions;
input x1-x10;
total = mean(of x1-x12);
y = (x1 + x2 + x3 + x4 + x5) * sqrt(x6);
complex = ((x1 + x2)/(x3 -1) * (x4 -1) + 2;
datalines;
1 2 3 4 5 -5 -4 -3 -2 -1
;
proc print;
run;
```

Exercise 3.2

```
input x1-x10;
f1 = ((x1 + x2)/(x3 - 1) * (x4 - 1) + 2
f2 = (x5 + x6)/(x7 - 1) * (x8 - 1)) + 2;
datalines;
1 2 3 4 5 -5 -4 -3 -2 -1
;
proc print;
run;
```

Logical Statements

Logical statements are extremely important features of any program language. They enable you to perform tasks on data or cases, contingent upon certain values or conditions in the data. The IF . . . THEN logical statement says to perform the command that follows the THEN portion of the statement only when the conditional statement following the IF is met or true. In prior examples the IF . . . THEN statement was used to output messages as either headers or footers for an output report, as in

```
IF _N_ = 1 THEN PUT 'This Is The First Case';
```

With this statement, the PUT statement is executed only when _N_ equals 1. Note that the conditional part of this statement involved a single variable (_N_) being equal to a given value (1). You can also specify that a variable must be equal to another variable, as in

```
IF _N_ = ID THEN PUT '_N_ Equals ID For This Case';
```

Conditional statements are not restricted to a variable being equal to a given value or another variable. Table 4.1 is a list of possible operators. You can use them within a statement with their symbols or abbreviations. The first is the Equal To, which you can specify by using its symbol, as in

```
IF _N_ = ID THEN PUT . . . ;
```

or its abbreviation EQ as in

```
IF _N_ EQ ID THEN PUT . . . ;
```

The second possibility shown in the table is the Not Equal To (NE). In this case, you specify that the variable is unequal to the value, as in

```
IF _N_ ^= 1 THEN PUT 'This Is Not The First Case';
```

This statement will print out for every case for which _N_ is not equal to 1. It will do the opposite of the statement using the Equal To by outputting for every case except the first one.

Conditional statements can use Greater Than (GT) and Less Than (LT), as in

```
IF _N_ < 2 THEN PUT 'Print The First Case';
```

or

```
IF _N_ > 1 THEN PUT 'Print All But The First Case';
```

The first example will print the message only for the first case because only the first case has an _N_ with a value less than 2. The second example will print the message for every case except the first one because every case except the first one has an _N_ with a value greater than 1.

You can also use Greater Than Or Equal To (GE) and Less Than Or Equal To (LE). The statement

```
IF _N_ >= 1 THEN PUT 'Print All Cases';
```

will print a message for every case because every case has an _N_ that is equal to 1 or is greater than 1.

It is possible to have multiple conditions in a statement. These are joined by an AND or an OR. The AND means that both conditions are met. The OR means that one condition or the other condition (or both conditions) is met. The statement

Table 4.1

SAS Logical Operators

Symbol	Abbreviation	Operation
=	EQ	Equal to
^= Or ~=	NE	Not equal to
>	GT	Greater than
<	LT	Less than
>= or =>	GE	Greater than or equal to
<= or =<	LE	Less than or equal to
&	AND	And
|	OR	Or

```
IF X = 1 AND Y = 1 THEN PUT . . . ;
```

will output for all cases in which both conditions are met. That is, X must be equal to 1 and Y must be equal to 1. **If** you use the **OR**, as in

```
IF X = 1 OR Y = 1 THEN PUT . . . ;
```

then outputting will be done for all cases in which either X or Y is equal to 1. It will also output for cases where both X and Y are equal to 1. Thus, it will output all cases output by the statement using the AND. Whereas in this example the cases output by the OR statement included all the cases output by the AND statement, this will not always occur.

You can also use AND and OR to specify multiple values for the same variable, as in

```
IF _N_ = 1 OR _N_ = 2 THEN PUT . . . ;
```

Here output will be done for the first and second cases only. Note that if we use AND with this statement:

```
IF _N_ = 1 AND _N_ = 2 THEN PUT . . . ;
```

no cases will be output. This is because a variable has a single value so _N_ cannot be equal to both 1 and 2. This is a logical error for which you will get no error message in your SAS Log. This is because it is a valid SAS statement, even though it is logically incorrect.

You can produce even more complex logical statements. Suppose you wish to choose cases for which X has a value of either 1 or 2, and at the same time Y has a value of 8. You could use the statement

```
IF (X = 1 OR X = 2) AND Y = 8 THEN . . . ;
```

Note the use of the parentheses to make it clear the order in which the ORs and ANDs should be considered. This is necessary when you mix ANDs and ORs because the above statement is not equivalent to

```
IF X = 1 OR (X = 2 AND Y = 8) THEN . . . ;
```

The latter example will pick up all cases with an X value equal to 1 regardless of the value for Y. The former example will pick up cases with an X value equal to 1 only if they have a Y value equal to 8. You must be very careful mixing ANDs and ORs to avoid logical errors.

A second area of potential confusion involves the specification of a range of values using AND or OR with Greater Than and Less Than. Suppose you have the numbers 1 to 10:

```
1 2 3 4 5 6 7 8 9 10.
```

You might wish to include all cases that fall within a range, say all cases between 4 and 7, inclusive (i.e., 4, 5, 6, 7). Conversely, you might wish to include all cases that fall outside of that range, that is, all cases less than 4 or greater than 7 (i.e., 1, 2, 3, 8, 9, 10). To specify the range between two numbers, use AND as in

```
IF X >= 4 AND X <= 7 THEN . . . ;
```

This statement says to consider all cases equal to or greater than 4 (i.e., 4, 5, 6, 7, 8, 9, 10) and all cases less than or equal to 7 (i.e., 7, 6, 5, 4, 3, 2, 1), then select only those cases that are in both lists (i.e., 4, 5, 6, 7). If you were to use an OR, you would take cases from both lists, which would be all the cases, since combined, both lists include every case.

To specify all cases outside the range, use the OR as in

```
IF X < 4 OR X > 7 THEN . . . ;
```

This time the statement says to take all cases less than 4 (i.e., 3, 2, 1) and all cases greater than 7 (i.e., 8, 9, 10) and select cases that fall in either list (i.e., 1, 2, 3, 8, 9, 10). Had you used an AND with this example, you would have selected no cases because no case has a value of X that is both less than 4 and greater than 7.

PROGRAM TO SCREEN
FOR DATA ERRORS

At every stage of data collection and data handling, errors invariably are introduced. Every data file must be carefully checked for errors. Some of these errors can be detected with a computer program that searches a data set for impossible or improbable values or combinations. For example, yes/no questions are often coded as 1 for yes and 0 for no. Any other value would be "out of range" and an error. Likewise, certain combinations can be impossible. For a sample of employees, you could have a variable of employee age and another of tenure on the job. It is not possible that a person 20 years old could have been working on the job for 25 years.

A program to search for data errors should begin by inputting data. It should then run a series of tests using logical statements to test for probable data errors. When an error is found, the program should output a statement noting the case number and error.

Program 4.1 is an example of a program that screens a data set for impossible values and combinations. For this example, data are entered for eight cases, each of which has three variables. The first variable is an identification number and is named ID. The second variable is age in years and is named AGE. The third variable (VOTER) is voter status where a value of 1 represents being a registered voter and a value of 2 represents not being a registered voter.

Program 4.1
Program to Screen for Data Errors

```
1 DATA SCREEN;
2    INPUT ID 1 AGE 2-3 VOTER 4;
3    FILE PRINT;
4    IF _N_=1 THEN PUT @15 'Report Of Probable Data Errors.' /;
5    IF AGE < 17 THEN PUT 'Case #' ID 'Has An Age Of ' AGE;
6    IF VOTER < 1 OR VOTER > 2 THEN PUT 'Case #' ID
7       'Has A Value For Voter Of ' VOTER;
8    IF AGE < 18 AND VOTER = 1 THEN PUT 'Case #' ID
9       'Has An Age Of ' AGE 'And Is A Voter';
10 DATALINES;
   1211
   2203
   3222
   4112
   5171
   6312
   7292
   8331
   ;
   RUN;
```

Assume that the sample is composed of college students. Suppose that the youngest student in the population is 17. One must be at least 18 to be a registered voter. All this information can be programmed so that a report is generated, listing cases with values out of range. For example, a case can have too young an age (less than 18), or a case can have a VOTER value that is not 1 or 2. A case can have an implausible combination, such as being a registered voter younger than 18.

Program 4.1 has these rules programmed and produces a report (see Output 4.1) of each case with the offending variable value or values. The first three lines of the program give the name SCREEN to the SAS data set, input the three variables, and direct output to print. Line 4 outputs the title of the report for only the first case. Line 5 produces a line of output only for cases with age under 18 that indicates the ID number of the case and the out of range value for age. Lines 6 and 7 test for an out of range value for VOTER (either greater than 2 or less than 1) and output the ID number and value for VOTER. Lines 8 and 9 test for cases that are less than 18 in age and are noted as voters.

Output 4.1

```
The SAS System

      Report Of Probable Data Errors.

Case #2 Has A Value For Voter Of 3
Case #4 Has An Age Of 11
Case #5 Has An Age Of 17 And Is A Voter
```

As can be seen in Output 4.1, three cases had out of range values or impossible combinations of values. Case #2 had a value of 3 for VOTER, case #4 had an age of 11, and case #5 was a registered voter who was 17 years of age.

THE ELSE STATEMENT

There are times when you may wish to do one thing with some of your cases and something else with the rest. This can be done with two IF . . . THEN statements, as in

```
IF Y = 1 THEN . . . ;
IF Y NE 1 THEN . . . ;
```

The ELSE statement can substitute for the second IF . . . THEN statement, as in

```
IF Y = 1 THEN . . . ;
ELSE . . . ;
```

The ELSE says to take all the cases not handled by the IF . . . THEN and do what follows the ELSE. Its function is to simplify your program. IF the first IF . . . THEN is complex, the second IF . . . THEN will be long and unwieldy. If your first IF . . . THEN were the following:

```
IF (X > 6 and X < 12) OR (Y = 1 AND Z = 10) THEN . . . ;
```

the ELSE would be far easier than figuring out how to specify all the remaining cases with an IF . . . THEN.

SELECTING AND DELETING CASES FROM A SAS DATA SET

Sometimes you want to select cases into or delete cases from the SAS data set being created by the data step. You can select cases that have or don't have a specified characteristic or set of characteristics. Conversely, you can delete cases that either have or don't have a particular characteristic or set of characteristics. The former operation is done with an IF . . . statement. The latter is done with the DELETE statement in conjunction with an IF . . . THEN.

Selection is done by specifying the condition or conditions on an IF . . . statement, as in

```
IF GENDER = 2;
IF ID >= 100;
IF ID >= 100 AND GENDER = 2;
```

The first example selects only cases that have gender values of 2. The second example selects only cases that have ID values equal to or greater than 100. The third example selects only cases that meet both conditions. Only cases meeting the specified conditions will be placed into the SAS data set.

The opposite operation is to delete cases for which the specified conditions on the IF . . . THEN are true. Each of the above examples could be accomplished with an opposite DELETE statement:

```
IF GENDER NE 2 THEN DELETE;
IF ID < 100 THEN DELETE;
IF GENDER NE 2 OR ID < 100 THEN DELETE;
```

Just as with DROP and KEEP, all cases having these specified characteristics will be dropped from the SAS data set once the data step is finished. If you input the current data set into another using the SET statement, save the data set as a SAS library, or if you run any PROC on the data set, these cases will be gone.

DETECTING THE END OF A FILE

In an earlier example an IF . . . THEN statement was used to output a message after the last case was input. To accomplish this, the number of cases was written into the program statement to allow outputting for the last case, which was noted by its number. In most applications, however, it is inconvenient to program the number of the last case. This is particularly true when your program is designed to be used for more than one data set. There is a feature, however, that allows your program to automatically detect when it has reached the end of an input data set.

The END= option is used on the INFILE statement to create a variable that tells your program when it has reached the last case in the file. The format of the statement is

```
INFILE 'data set name' END = variable name
```

where "data set name" is the name of the data set to be input and "variable name" is a name given to the variable that will carry the information about the end of the file. In Program 4.2 the file end detector is named ENDFILE, that is,

```
INFILE 'EX42.DAT' END = ENDFILE;
```

ENDFILE in this example is a variable that has a value for every case. It is automatically given a value of 0 for all cases but the last one, for which it is given a value of 1. To detect the end of the file, you can use an IF statement to test if the value of the variable is 1, as in

```
IF ENDFILE = 1 THEN PUT 'This is the Last Case';
```

There is a shorthand way to test ENDFILE with the IF statement. It is not necessary to use the "= 1". Rather, you can use the statement:

```
IF ENDFILE THEN . . .
```

The direction following the THEN will be executed only when ENDFILE is equal to 1. If it is not equal to 1, the statement will not be executed.

EXECUTING SEVERAL STATEMENTS AFTER AN IF . . . THEN

Sometimes you execute a series of statements after an IF . . . THEN. For example, you might wish to do a series of calculations and output a report after the last case is input. You could put each statement that you wish to carry out after an IF ENDFILE THEN. . . . Alternately, you can define a group of statements to be executed following a single IF . . . THEN by means of a IF . . . THEN DO . . . END.

With this statement, when the statement following the **IF** is true, every statement between the **DO** and **END** is executed, as in:

```
IF _N_ = 1 THEN DO;
  PUT 'This is the First Case.';
  PUT 'This Message Will Print for the First Case';
  PUT 'Every Statement Will Be Carried Out Until the
  END';
  END;
```

For the first case only, the three statements will be output. Note the indenting of the statements between the DO and END. It is easier to follow and debug a program when statements between the DO and END are indented.

OVERRIDING CASE-BY-CASE RESETTING OF VARIABLE VALUES

The SAS language begins each case with all variable values set equal to "missing." When a case is input, all variables are assigned missing values, which are replaced with the inputted values for each case. If data are missing, the value for the missing variable remains missing. Variables not contained on an INPUT statement must be defined within the program with expressions or functions. Sometimes, however, you might wish to keep the values of a variable from case to case. The RETAIN statement overrides the automatic resetting of variables. To do so, you must list the variables that you do not want reset.

For example, suppose you wish to accumulate the sum of a variable from case to case. The variable that you wish to sum will be named X, and the variable that contains the sum will be named SUMX. To prevent SUMX from resetting for each case, use the statement

```
RETAIN SUMX 0;
```

Now for each case you can add the value of **X** to the running total **SUMX** with a statement

```
SUMX = SUMX + X;
```

For each case X will be added to the value of SUMX that is pending from the prior case.

For the sum to accumulate properly, you must give SUMX the appropriate starting value. In this example, when the first case is executed, you want SUMX to have a value of 0. Thus, after the statement is executed for the first case, SUMX will equal X, or SUMX is equal to 0 plus the value of X for case #1.

Giving a variable a starting value is termed initialization. Initialization is accomplished within the RETAIN statement by putting the starting value after the variable name, as in

```
RETAIN SUMX 0;
```

It is possible to list several variables on a RETAIN statement, and it is possible to give different starting values to different variables. For example:

```
RETAIN SUMX SUMY 0 A B C 1 XY 2;
```

This statement says that six variables are to have the automatic reset overridden. SUMX and SUMY are to have starting values of 0; A, B, and C are to have starting values of 1; and XY is to have a starting value of 2.

ACCUMULATORS AND COUNTERS

Two frequent tasks to accomplish within a program are accumulating and counting across cases. The example in the prior section on RETAIN statements illustrates the use of an **accumulator**. An accumulator is a variable that aggregates values of a variable over cases or several variables within a case. In the prior example, SUMX was an accumulator variable that contains the sum of a variable across cases. It is also possible to accumulate functions other than sums. In statistics, it is common to accumulate sums of observations squared. In other words, you square the observations for a variable and sum them across cases.

Counters are used to count the number of cases or the number of times an operation is carried out. You might wish to count the number of cases that contain a certain characteristic. A statement such as

```
IF CHARACT = 1 THEN N = N + 1;
```

says to count the number of cases with a value of 1 for CHARACT.

Expanding on the above example, you can write a program to select certain cases and calculate their mean on a variable. This would involve using the following SAS statements:

```
INPUT TEST X;
RETAIN SUMX N 0;
IF TEST = 1 THEN DO;
   SUMX = SUMX + X;
   N = N + 1;
END;
MEANX = SUMX / N;
```

These statements, which might be part of a complete program, say to add the values of X for cases with a value for TEST of 1. They also say to count the number of cases that are summed with the N = N + 1 statement. Finally, the last statement says to calculate the mean of X using the calculated value of SUMX and N.

COMPUTING AN INDEPENDENT GROUP *t* TEST

One of the major purposes of a SAS program is to conduct statistical tests. Although most common tests are available in PROCs, occasionally you may need to conduct a test that is not available in a PROC. Program 4.2 uses features discussed in this chapter to compute an independent group *t* test, which can also be conducted with a PROC.

There are three basic steps to computing a *t* test. First, the necessary terms must be computed. These are the sum, mean, sum of squares, and sample size, computed for each of the two groups separately. Then the necessary terms are used to compute the value of *t*. Finally, the results must be outputted.

This program has three major blocks of statements. One block calculates the necessary terms for the first group of cases, another block calculates the necessary terms for the second group of cases, and a third block calculates the *t* test itself and outputs a report. As cases are processed one by one, not every block of statements is carried out for every case. The first block is carried out only for cases that belong to the first group, the second block is only carried out for cases that belong to the second group, and the last block is only carried out after all cases have been read.

The logic of this program is more complex than those we've seen up to this point. To help see the structure of the program, a flowchart is provided (see Figure 4.1). The first step is to read the data for a case. If the case is from the first group, the block of statements that computes the first group necessary terms is executed. If the case is from the second group, the block of statements that computes the second group necessary terms is executed. If the current case being processed is not the last one in the file, then another case is read and the procedure is repeated. When the last case has been encountered, the program executes the final block of statements, which computes the *t* test and outputs a report.

For the program tasks to be carried out, the file must contain one independent and one dependent variable, named GROUP and DV, respectively, in this example. IF . . . THEN DO . . . END statements are used to separately compute the necessary terms across cases for each group separately, and to compute the value of *t* from the necessary terms.

Program 4.2
Program to Compute a *t* Test

```
1   DATA TTEST;
2   INFILE 'EX42.DAT' END = ENDFILE;
3   INPUT GROUP 1 DV 2-3;
4   RETAIN NA NB SUMA SUMB SUMA2 SUMB2 MEANA MEANB SSA SSB 0;
5    ********************Calculate Basic Quantities for t-test;
6   IF GROUP = 1 THEN DO;
7     NA = NA + 1;      *Sample Size;
8     SUMA = SUMA + DV;      *Sum of DV;
9     SUMA2 = SUMA2 + DV**2;      *Sum of DV Squared;
10    MEANA = SUMA/NA;      *Mean;
11    SSA = SUMA2 - (SUMA**2/NA);      *Sum of Squares;
12  END;
13  IF GROUP = 2 THEN DO;
14    NB = NB + 1;      *Sample Size;
15    SUMB = SUMB + DV;      *Sum of DV;
16    SUMB2 = SUMB2 + DV**2;      *Sum of DV Squared;
17    MEANB = SUMB/NB;      *Mean;
18    SSB = SUMB2 - (SUMB**2/NB);      *Sum of Squares;
19  END;
20  IF ENDFILE THEN DO;
21    ********************Compute standard deviations;
22    SDA = SQRT(SSA/NA);
23    SDB = SQRT(SSB/NB);
24    ********************Calculate t-test and probability of t;
25    T = (MEANA-MEANB)/SQRT((SSA+SSB)/(NA+NB-2)* (1/NA+1/NB));
26    IF T > 0 then TP = -1 * T;
27    ELSE TP = T;
28    MEANA = ROUND (MEANA,.1); MEANB = ROUND (MEANB,.1);
29    DF = NA + NB - 2;
30    PT = 2 * ROUND(PROBT(TP,DF),.0001);
31    ********************Print Report;
32    FILE PRINT;
33    PUT @15 'Independent Group T-Test' /;
34    PUT 'Mean For Group A = ' MEANA;
35    PUT 'Mean For Group B = ' MEANB;
36    PUT 'Standard Deviation For Group A = ' SDA;
37    PUT 'Standard Deviation For Group B = ' SDB;
38    PUT;
39    PUT 'T With ' DF 'Degrees Of Freedom = ' T;
40    PUT 'Two-Tailed Probability of T = ' PT;
41    IF PT > .05 THEN PUT / @20 'T Is Significant!';
42    IF PT <= .05 THEN PUT / @20 'T Is Nonsignificant!';
43  END;
44  RUN;
```

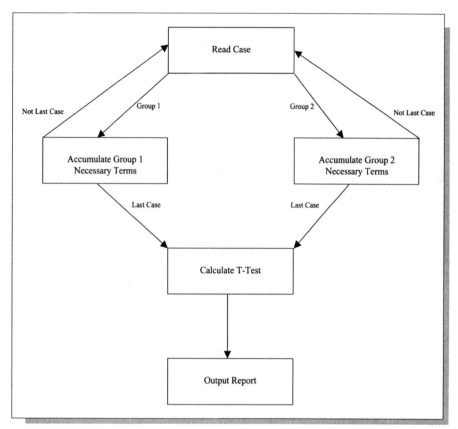

Figure 4.1. Flowchart for Program 4.2

As you can see in the program listing, data are input from an external file named EX42.DAT (see line 2). The END= feature was placed on the INFILE statement so that final computations and a report could be done for only the last case. ENDFILE is the name of the variable assigned to contain information about when the last case was input.

The RETAIN statement (line 4) indicates that 10 variables are to retain their values from case to case, and that all are to be initialized to 0. The first two variables on the RETAIN statement are counters (NA and NB). The remaining variables are accumulators. These are not distinguished in the RETAIN statement.

The block of statements following the first comment (lines 6 to 12) accumulate the terms necessary for a *t* test for group 1. As you can see, if GROUP has a value of 1, then this block of statements following the DO is executed. NA is the number of cases, SUMA is the sum of DV, SUMA2 is the sum of DV squared, MEANA is the mean of DV, and SSA is the sum of squares of DV, using the formula

$$SS = \Sigma(X - M)^2,$$

where X is a value of the variable X and M is the mean of the observations.

The next block of statements (lines 13 to 19) does the same thing as the first group, but for the second group of cases, where GROUP equals 2.

After the final case is read, the value for *t* and final report are produced. Note the IF ENDFILE THEN DO statement (line 20). The remainder of the program is executed only once, for the final case. First standard deviations for each group are computed in lines 22 and 23. Next, T is computed using an expression (line 25). The values for the two group means are rounded to one digit to the right of the decimal using the ROUND function (line 28). Note that there are two statements on this line. The degrees of freedom are calculated on line 29. The two-tailed probability for the calculated *t* is computed with the PROBT function (line 30). A negative sign is put in front of positive *t* values in line 26 so that the function will return the one-tailed significance level for the lower tail, which is doubled in line 30. The ELSE statement in line 27 sets TP equal to T when T is positive.

Finally, a report is generated (lines 32 to 42) that outputs the means for both groups, the standard deviations for both groups, the *t* value with its degrees of freedom, and the exact probability that a *t* this extreme or larger would be observed by chance under the null hypothesis. The last two IF statements (lines 41 and 42) say to output a final message noting whether or not the *t* was significant at the $p < .05$ level. If the observed value of *t* has a probability less than the critical value of .05, the message "T Is Significant!" is output. If the probability is equal to or greater than .05, the message "T Is Nonsignificant!" is output.

The output from this program is shown in Output 4.2. Note that the values for the standard deviations and the *t* test contain more significant digits than you would probably want. This is because they were not rounded.

This program can be used with minimal modification on any data set that contains an independent and a dependent variable. The name of the data set

Output 4.2

```
The SAS System
                Independent Group T-Test
Mean For Group A = 20
Mean For Group B = 28.6
Standard Deviation For Group A = 2.9760952366
Standard Deviation For Group B = 5.1224993899

T With 11 Degrees Of Freedom = -3.341475563
Two-Tailed Probability of T = 0.0074

                T Is Significant!
```

and format for the variables need to be entered on the INFILE and INPUT statements. The program assumes that the independent variable has values of 1 and 2 for the different groups. Modifications could be made to have the program do more than one *t* test if multiple independent or dependent variables were placed in a file. Of course, it would be easier to conduct your *t* tests with a PROC rather than writing your own program. (Chapter 9 shows how this is done with PROC TTEST.) The PROC can be very helpful in testing your program to be sure it is computing the statistic correctly. For a statistical test that is not found in a PROC, you must write your own procedure.

COMMON ERRORS

It is easy to make mistakes with logic statements, especially if they are complex and involve more than one condition or more than one variable. As we noted earlier, it is possible to create conditions that are either always true or always false by mixing up the AND and OR operators. Be sure to test your logic statements, and in particular test all possible combinations. Sometimes some combinations will work correctly and others will not.

When working with accumulators and counters, perhaps the most common error is to forget needed variables on the RETAIN, or to forget the entire statement. This will result in your variables resetting for each case, and the final values will either be missing or based on only the final case.

∼ Debugging Exercises ∼

Exercise 4.1

```
   *Purpose of the program is to compute a
mean of all subjects on height;
   data logic;
   input gender height;
   retain sumheight 0;
   if gender = 1 and gender = 2;
     n = n + 1;
     sumheight = height;
     meanheight = sumheight/n;
   datalines;
   1 68
   1 74
   1 70
   1 72
   1 75
   2 66
   2 64
   2 66
   2 64
   ;
   proc print;
   run;
```

Exercise 4.2

```
   *Purpose of the program is to compute a
separate mean for males and females;
  data logic;
  input gender $ height;
  retain sumheightm sumheightf nm nf 0;
  if gender = m then do;
    sumheightm = sumheightm + height;
    nm = nm + 1;
  end;
  if gender = f then do;
    sumheghtf = sumheightf + height;
    nf = nf + 1;
  end;
  file print;
  if _n_ = 9 then do;
  meanm = sumheightm/nf;
  meanf = sumheightf/nm;
    put 'mean for males (inches) = ' meanm
@40 'mean for females (inches) = ' meanf;
  end;
  datalines;
  m 68
  m 74
  m 70
  m 72
  m 75
  f 66
  f 64
  f 66
  f 64
  ;
  run;
```

Chapter 5

Branching With GOTO and LINK

So far all the example programs have involved a fixed order of statements, where each statement is executed once and only once for each case. Many applications, however, require more complex programming where each case may involve a different set of statements that processes it. The *t* test program (Program 4.2) from Chapter 4 is an example, where the group 1 cases were handled by one block of statements and the group 2 cases were handled by another. Certain statements were executed only for the last case in the file. To accomplish many tasks, you must take control of the order of execution of statements. Such control can be accomplished by means of the GOTO and LINK statements. These statements say to skip from one statement to another that may occur several statements later, or prior to the current statement. You can also say to skip to different portions of your program, depending on values of one or more variables. Skipping to different sections contingent on some predetermined condition is called branching.

GOTO STATEMENT

The GOTO or GO TO statement says to skip to a specified statement and continue processing. It is used in conjunction with a label that marks the destination for a GOTO statement. For example, the statement

```
GOTO ALBL;
```

says to skip to the statement that has the label ALBL. The label is a single string of characters that is followed by a colon, as in

```
ALBL:
```

It can be placed on a line by itself, or it can be followed by another statement, as in

```
ALBL: PUT 'I Have Skipped To ALBL';
```

Valid names for labels follow the same rules as valid names for variables. A label name can be up to eight characters (letters, numbers, and underscores, "_") long, and it must begin with a letter or an underscore.

Used together, the GOTO and label enable you to skip statements, typically based on some condition, as in the following:

```
IF _N_ = 1 THEN GOTO LBL;
(Other Statements Go Here)
LBL: PUT 'This Is The First Case';
```

GOTOs allow you to skip from one statement to another, but your computer will continue relentlessly to execute statement after statement. Statements that are skipped might never be executed in a particular run of a program. Other statements might be executed multiple times if your program directs the computer to do so. The SAS System does not keep track of what has and has not been executed, so once you take control of the order of execution, you must be careful that everything gets executed in the proper order. When you skip around, your programming task will become more difficult and complex. For this reason, you should avoid using the GOTO statement unless absolutely necessary.

LINK STATEMENT

The LINK statement is much like a GOTO except that it says to skip to a block of statements and to return to the statement following the LINK when the block is completed. By returning to the place from where it was called, the LINK makes for more orderly programs than the GOTO. Proper use of LINK makes the programming task easier by facilitating keeping track of the logical flow of your program.

The block of statements called by the LINK statement begins with a label and ends with a RETURN statement. Every statement between the label and the RETURN is executed. Then the program skips to the statement following the LINK statement. This is illustrated in the following sequence of statements:

```
FILE PRINT;
LINK LABELA;
   PUT 'This Statement Is Printed Third.';
   LABELA: PUT 'This Statement Is Printed First.';
   PUT 'This Statement Is Printed Second.';
RETURN;
```

The LINK instructs the computer to skip to the label LABELA. The PUT statement will output the "Printed First" statement, and then the "Printed Second" statement. The RETURN statement redirects to the statement immediately following the LINK statement. In this case, it is the PUT with the "Printed Third" message. With the program as written here, the computer will continue to execute the statements in order, and it will execute the "Printed First" and "Printed Second" statements a second time. To override this, you must put a statement before the LABELA statement to direct the computer to another part of the program, to stop processing the present case and input the next case (with a RETURN statement), or to stop the program (with a STOP statement).

RETURN STATEMENT

We have just seen how the RETURN statement sends execution back to the statement following a LINK statement. There is another use of the RETURN statement that instructs the computer to input the next case without executing the remaining statements in the data step. This presumes, of course, that the program is inputting data into the data step. A RETURN is automatically assumed after the last statement of a data step is executed. The next case is automatically inputted, as has occurred in several of the prior examples. Once you take control of the order of execution, it may become necessary to indicate when to input the next case.

In the prior example, a RETURN could be placed before the LABELA statement to direct the program to stop processing the current case and read the next case. This will prevent printing the first two statements a second time.

STOP STATEMENT

The STOP statement says to stop the program without inputting any more cases. This is particularly useful in programs that don't input data, such as Program 5.1. With the above example, if you were not inputting data, you could put a STOP before LABELA to stop the data step without printing the first two statements twice. You must be careful when using the STOP statement that everything you wish done has been, and that outputting has been completed. It is a common error when using STOP to omit the outputting of the last case. The STOP statement is illustrated in Program 5.1 and Program 5.2.

OUTPUT STATEMENT REVISITED

Chapter 2 discussed the use of OUTPUT to output a line of data to a SAS data set. In Program 2.1, multiple OUTPUT statements outputted the same line more than once. OUTPUT can become necessary when you take control of the order of statement execution so that you can indicate when to output. There are times when variables will not have their values added to the data set created by the data step unless you specifically use an OUTPUT statement in the appropriate place. This will be illustrated in Program 5.2.

Program 5.1

```
1    DATA FINDHER;
2    INPUT GENDER 1. NAME $8.;
3    RETAIN FIRSTFL 0;
4    IF FIRSTFL = 0 AND GENDER = 2 THEN LINK FOUND;
5    RETURN;
6    STOP;
7    FOUND:
8        FILE PRINT;
9        PUT 'First Female Manager Was ' NAME;
10       FIRSTFL = 1;
11   RETURN;
DATALINES;
1BOB
1JOHN
1TOM
1AL
2JANE
1HARRY
2CAROL
1RICHARD
2ANN
;
RUN;
```

FLAGS

A flag is a device that allows a program to keep track of the status or state of a variable or set of variables. It is used in places where you may wish to execute a block of statements only when some condition or conditions are met. Alternately, you may wish to execute different blocks of statements, depending on the condition or conditions existing at the time.

The flag itself is a variable that can take on two or more values. If you wish to keep track of whether or not a particular condition is in force, you can define a flag variable to have one value, typically 1, when the condition is met, and another value, typically 0, when the condition is not met. Thus you "raise the flag" to indicate that something has occurred or is in force. This is useful when you wish to keep track of a condition across cases. In other words, you may wish to keep track of variables from prior cases. The flag stays at its present value until the program resets it to another.

For example, suppose you wish to locate in a file the date for the first female middle manager hired in a company that at one time had a history of not hiring women. If a data file exists that includes gender and date of employment, and if the file is sorted according to date hired, a flag can be used to help identify the first female.

To accomplish this, you set a flag initially to be equal to zero by using a RETAIN. Then, as you read case by case, you test to see if you have yet found a female (remember that the file is sorted by date of hiring). When your program encounters the first female case, the flag will have a value of 0, and you instruct the computer to output whatever information is in the file on that case. You also reset the flag to equal 1. For all other female cases encountered, the flag will equal 1, which identifies them as not being the first.

How this is done can be seen in Program 5.1, which searches through several cases and outputs the name of the first female encountered. For illustrative purposes, data were placed after the DATALINES statement inside the program. As can be seen, there are nine employees, six male and three female. Jane is the first female, so the program will output a single line that indicates this.

The program inputs two variables, GENDER and NAME (line 2). The flag, FIRSTFL, is initialized to 0 by the RETAIN statement (line 3). Line 4 is an IF statement that detects when the first female manager is encountered. This occurs when a case's value for GENDER is 2, meaning that the case is female, and FIRSTFL still has a value of 0, meaning that a female has not yet been encountered. When the fifth case is processed, the two conditions on line 4 will be met, and processing is sent to the label FOUND. A single line of output will be sent to the print location, indicating the first female's name (lines 8 and 9). The value for the flag is then set equal to 1 (line 10), indicating that the first female has been found. No other names will be output because the two conditions in line 4 will not again be met. The RETURN in line 11 sends execution to line 5. The RETURN sends execution back to the beginning, where another case is input. If the RETURN were missing, the STOP would be executed after the first case was input, and the program would not process the entire list of employees.

When the last case has been processed, execution falls through the RETURN, and the STOP is executed. If the STOP were not here, the program would execute lines 8 to 10 again.

The program outputs the single line:

```
First Female Manager Was JANE
```

Because this was the only line output, it was not necessary to have the program continue to read the file. Had the STOP statement been placed after line 9, the program would have output the message and stopped.

A MORE COMPLEX EXAMPLE OF STATEMENT CONTROL

Program 5.2 is a more complex illustration of the features discussed in this chapter. Its problem involves dividing a sample into two equal portions and then computing means for each portion. This program can be adapted for cross-validation with multiple regression analysis to split off a holdout sample. It places every other case in each group, which is a procedure frequently used for cross-validation. Then one multiple regression analysis can be done on the first half of the data, and a second can be done to see if the results are comparable.

The program uses LINKs and a flag, and it controls the outputting and returning. It was designed to read the data set from Program 4.2, for which a *t* test program was written. This time, rather than dividing the sample according to values of an independent variable, the sample is divided into the odd and even cases. Beginning with the first case, every other case is put into the odd category, and beginning with the second case, every other case is put into the even category. Means are computed for each of the two groups separately.

As you can see, the first three lines name the SAS data set ODDEVEN and input the variable DV from each case in the data set EX42.DAT. The fourth line initializes the flag FLAGOE, the counters that keep track of the number of cases in each group (NEVEN and NODD), and the accumulators for the sum of DV for each group (SUME and SUMO).

Program 5.2

```
1   DATA ODDEVEN;
2   INFILE 'EX42.DAT' END = FILEEND;
3   INPUT DV 2-3;
4   RETAIN FLAGOE NEVEN NODD SUME SUMO 0;
5   FLAGOE = 1 - FLAGOE;
6   IF FLAGOE = 0 THEN LINK EVEN;
7   IF FLAGOE = 1 THEN LINK ODD;
8   OUTPUT;
9   IF FILEEND THEN LINK REPORT;
10  IF FILEEND THEN STOP;
11  RETURN;
12  EVEN: *Accumulate even cases;
13     SUME = SUME + DV;
14     NEVEN = NEVEN + 1;
15  RETURN;
16  ODD: *Accumulate odd cases;
17     SUMO = SUMO + DV;
18     NODD = NODD + 1;
19  RETURN;
20  REPORT: *Calculate means and Print Report;
21     MEANE = SUME / NEVEN;
22     MEANO = SUMO / NODD;
23     FILE PRINT;
24     PUT 'Mean of Even Cases = ' MEANE;
25     PUT 'Mean of Odd Cases = ' MEANO;
26  RETURN;
27  PROC PRINT;
28  RUN;
```

The fifth line sets the flag for each case. To place cases alternately into the odd and even groups, a flag is used that alternates values back and forth with each case, in this case between a value of 1 and a value of 0. The expression FLAGOE = 1 − FLAGOE returns of value of 1 when the prior value of FLAGOE is 0, and it returns a value of 0 when the prior value of FLAGOE is 1. Because

FLAGOE is initialized to the value of 0, the first case is assigned a flag value of 1. The IF statements in lines 6 and 7 send execution to different subsections of the program, depending on the value of the flag. When the flag has a value of 0, the program links to the section labeled EVEN (line 12). When the flag has a value of 1, the program links to the section labeled ODD (line 16).

The subsection beginning with the label EVEN accumulates the sum of DVs for the even cases and counts the number of even cases. Note that it ends with a RETURN statement. The subsection beginning with the label ODD accumulates the sum of DVs for the odd cases and counts the number of odd cases.

Each subsection returns execution to the statement following the one that sent it there. For the even cases, execution returns to line 7. Because the flag is equal to 0, line 7 is not executed, and execution continues with the statement in line 8. For every odd case, execution returns to the statement in line 8. This statement controls when the case is output. The OUTPUT statement is necessary to output a line after each case is processed. If the OUTPUT statement were not here, all calculated values for the last case would not be output. The statement in line 9 tests to see if the case is the last one. If it is, execution is directed to the subsection beginning with the label REPORT (line 20). This section calculates the means for both groups and outputs a report. It returns execution to the 10th statement, which says to stop execution when the final case has been processed. Without this statement, execution would continue until the last statement of the program. The RETURN statement in the 11th line says to read the next case after each case has been processed. It is skipped for the last case because the program stops execution before it reaches line 11.

Output 5.2 shows the results of the PUT statements, which printed the means for both groups. A PROC PRINT was also run to illustrate what was going on with the variables from case to case. The first column of the table produced by the PROC PRINT shows the observation number. As you can see, there were 12 cases. The second column shows the inputted value for DV. The third column shows the values for FLAGOE, which flip-flopped from 1 to 0 across cases. The next two columns show the values for the counters, NEVEN and NODD. Because the flag for the first case was a 1, the program assigned DV to the odd group. NODD was incremented to 1, while NEVEN remained at 0. For case 2, NEVEN is incremented to 1, while NODD remains at 1. As you can see, NODD and NEVEN are incremented, first one then the other, from case to case. Columns 6 and 7 show the summing of the DVs for the odd

Output 5.2

Results of FILE PRINT

The SAS System

Mean of Even Cases = 25.333333333
Mean of Odd Cases = 21.833333333

Results of PROC PRINT

The SAS System

OBS	DV	FLAGOE	NEVEN	NODD	SUME	SUMO	MEANE	MEANO
1	26	1	0	1	0	26	.	.
2	21	0	1	1	21	26	.	.
3	18	1	1	2	21	44	.	.
4	17	0	2	2	38	44	.	.
5	18	1	2	3	38	62	.	.
6	22	0	3	3	60	62	.	.
7	18	1	3	4	60	80	.	.
8	38	0	4	4	98	80	.	.
9	26	1	4	5	98	106	.	.
10	24	0	5	5	122	106	.	.
11	25	1	5	6	122	131	.	.
12	30	0	6	6	152	131	.	.

and even groups. For the first case, the DV value of 26 is assigned to SUMO, while SUME remains at 0. For the second case, the DV value of 21 is assigned to SUME, while SUMO remains at 26. Case by case, first SUMO and then SUME have the value of DV added to them. The last two variables show missing values of "." for the means, MEANE and MEANO. These means are computed only after the last case has been output; hence, the means were never outputted into the SAS data set and show as missing in the PROC PRINT.

PROGRAM FLOW

Once you begin to use branching procedures, you must become far more careful about the flow of statements. Remember that the computer continues relentlessly to execute statement after statement. When you direct execution to another portion of the program, the computer continues to execute statement after statement. Thus, you must be careful that the program does what you expect it to do in the order you wish it done.

In planning your program, it is helpful to diagram what needs to be done. You can make a flowchart-type diagram to illustrate flow from section to section of the program. Figure 5.1 shows a flowchart for Program 5.2. The boxes represent different portions of the program and contain brief descriptions, some in pseudocode statements. The arrows represent the flow of statements from box to box. As you can see, each case is input, and the flag value is set. IF statements direct the program to the EVEN or ODD subsections. All cases are output. If the case is not the last one in the file, the computer is directed to read the next case. When the last case is read, the computer is directed to the REPORT section and to stop execution.

Another thing that you should learn to do with your programs is to execute them mentally. This involves reading each statement and thinking about what it accomplishes. It is helpful to do this exercise with a piece of paper so that you can keep track of what happens to the values of variables as you trace through the program. For programs that branch depending on values of variables, you should mentally execute cases that represent different possibilities. In Program 5.2, you should go through several cases to see what happens as you execute the even and odd cases.

Another consideration with complex programs that branch is the organization of the statements. It is helpful to separate the subsections of a program from the main section, rather than mixing them together. One advantage of the LINK over the GOTO statement is that it returns execution to the statement immediately following the LINK statement. Of course, you can accomplish the same thing with GOTOs by placing a label after each GOTO and directing execution to these labels after the subsections are executed.

Notice that Program 5.2 is organized into a main portion and subportions. The main portion contains a series of IF . . . THEN statements with LINKs, as well

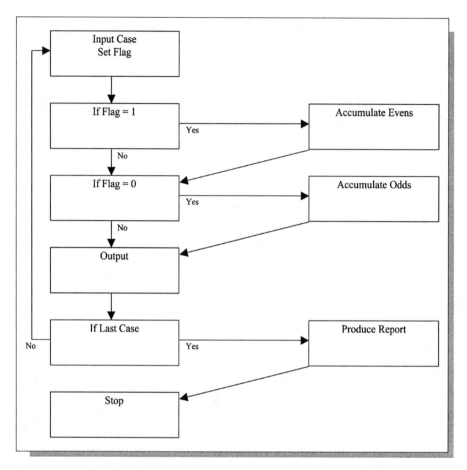

Figure 5.1. Flowchart for Program 5.2

as statements saying when to output results to the SAS data set, when to input the next case, and when to stop the program. The subsections that begin with labels and end with RETURNS are placed in order at the bottom of the program. This sort of organization generally is preferred because it makes tracing and debugging a program easier. This is because each subsection returns to the place from where it was called. Had the program been written so that it linked from inside subsections, it would have been far more difficult to trace the order of execution. The organization is also reflected in the flowchart in Figure 5.1. The boxes in the left-hand column of the figure are from the main section of the program. The boxes in the rightmost column are from the subsections.

It is not always possible to keep this sort of structure and to avoid linking within subsections of programs. Sometimes subsections are designed to decide which other subsections to link to, depending on the outcome of some calculations or tests. When branching becomes very complex, it may become necessary to have links within subsections. Avoid the temptation to do this unless absolutely necessary. If used to the extreme, it produces what programmers call **spaghetti code**. If you were to take a listing of your program and draw arrows from statement to statement where branching occurs, you would have what looks like a mass of spaghetti. With the approach suggested here, your program would produce a flowchart that looks like Figure 5.1. Spaghetti code would produce a flowchart that looks more like Figure 5.2. This sort of structure would be difficult to write a program from because it is difficult to trace the flow of statements.

COMMON ERRORS

Branching greatly increases the potential for logical errors. This is why it is so important to keep your programs well organized and to avoid spaghetti code. If your test run detects an error in a calculation, it can be almost impossible to trace through the program and find the error if the program is complex and disorganized. It will also be difficult to run tests because it will be hard to determine where to insert the PUT commands. With a well-organized program, you can insert a PUT after each section and readily trace where problems occur.

There are four things in particular to be careful of with branching. First, be sure that the conditions you specify for the branching are properly stated. All the problems with IF statements discussed in the prior chapter are relevant here. Second, be sure the program is redirected properly after the branching occurs. As noted earlier, it is easy to send SAS to a later part of the program to accomplish something and then have it continue to execute every other statement in the program even though it shouldn't. Be careful what gets executed after SAS returns to the statement immediately following a LINK. Third, be careful with the RETURN statement. Once it is executed, the next case will be read, so be sure all computations have been done for the current case. Fourth, once you use an OUTPUT statement in the program, you must maintain control over when data for every case gets put into the SAS data set. It is very common to overlook that the OUTPUT is not being executed for every case and wind up

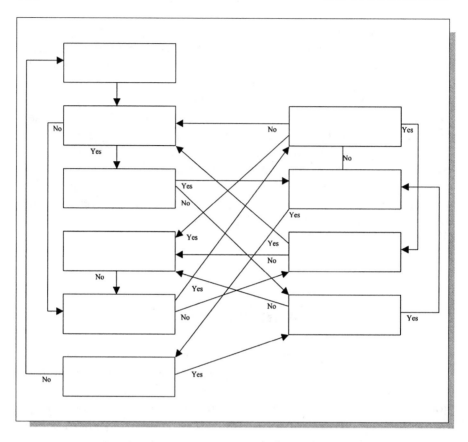

Figure 5.2. Flowchart of Program Written in Spaghetti Code

with too few cases. On the other hand, be sure the OUTPUT doesn't get executed too many times, as you can wind up with duplicate cases. Finally, be careful not to create a program that will never end. It is possible to create an endless loop where the program jumps from place to place in a circle and never ends. If this happens, you can terminate the program by clicking on the icon that is an exclamation mark ("!") in a circle on the right-hand portion of the menu bar near the top of the screen for Release 8.01, or on the X icon in the upper right-hand corner of the screen. You will get a dialog box that asks if you wish to terminate SAS or just the current program.

∽ *Debugging Exercises* ∽

Exercise 5.1

```
   Purpose of the program is to count the number
of people who are under 72 inches tall;
   data logic;
   input gender height;
   retain shortn 0;
   if height < 72 then link count;
   if _n_ = 9 then link report;
   count:
   shortn = shortn + 1;
   return;
   report:
   file print;
     put 'number of people under six feet tall = '
shortn;
   return;
   data;
   1 68
   2 74
   3 70
   4 72
   5 75
   6 66
   7 64
   8 66
   9 64
   ;
   run;
```

Exercise 5.2

```
  *Purpose of the program is to compute a
separate mean for males and females using
link statements;
  data logic
  input gender $ height;
  retain sumheightm sumheightf nm nf 0;
  if gender = 'm' then link male;
  if gender = 'f' then link female;
  if _n_ = 9 then link means;
  male: sumheightm = sumheightm + height;
    nm = nm + 1;
  female: sumheightf = sumheightf + height;
    nf = nf + 1;
  return;
  means;
    meanm = sumheightm/nm;
    meanf = sumheightf/nf;
    file print;
    put 'mean for males (inches) = ' meanm @40
'mean for females (inches) = ' meanf;
  return;
  datalines;
  m 68
  m 74
  m 70
  m 72
  m 75
  f 66
  f 64
  f 66
  f 64
  ;
  run;
```

Chapter 6

Do Loops

You have already seen how a DO . . . END statement can be used to execute a series of statements when it follows an IF . . . THEN statement. This chapter will discuss the use of the DO to repeat or iterate a block of statements. The various DOs enable you to write programs more efficiently by allowing execution of a block of statements a specified number of times or when certain conditions are met. This saves the trouble of repeating statements or of using IF statements to test for certain conditions.

A common use of DO statements is to generate a series of random numbers from a distribution with known characteristics. This could be used, for example, to produce a sample of 10 observations from a normal distribution for a class problem or exam. The generation of random numbers is at the heart of computer simulations or Monte Carlo studies, which can be used to explore the behavior of statistical tests under certain conditions, such as when assumptions are violated. This chapter contains an example of a program that demonstrates the Type 1 error rate of the independent *t* test when the assumption of homogeneity of variance is violated. The writing of this program was made quite efficient by the use of DO statements.

Three types of DO statements will be discussed—the DO Index=, the DO UNTIL, and the DO WHILE. The DO Index= allows you to create a Do loop that will iterate a block of statements a specified number of times. The DO UNTIL says to execute a block of statements until a specified condition occurs.

The DO WHILE says to execute a block of statements until a specified condition is no longer true. In all cases, the block of statements begins immediately following the DO statement and is ended by an END statement.

DO INDEX=

The DO Index= statement allows you to specify the number of iterations that a loop will execute. Following the equal sign, you place a range of numbers that represents the number of iterations. This chapter will deal with ranges that begin with 1 and are incremented by 1 for each iteration. The next chapter, on arrays, will introduce DOs that begin with other numbers and increment by numbers other than 1.

The DO Index= can specify a range of numbers, as in

```
DO I = 1 TO 10;
```

or it can specify a range from 1 to a variable, as in

```
DO I = 1 TO K;
```

In the former case, the loop will iterate 10 times; in the latter, it will iterate K times, where the program specifies the value of K. I is the **index variable**, the values of which are defined by the DO statement. It is not necessary to use I, although I is frequently used by programmers as the name for an index variable in a DO statement. Any valid variable name can be used for the index variable. The statement

```
DO POLICY = 1 to 15;
```

is a valid one.

The Do loop says to begin by assigning the leftmost value to the index variable. In this chapter, the index always begins at 1, and on each iterative execution of the loop, the index is incremented by 1. The procedure continues until the rightmost value for the index is achieved. Because the index is a variable, it will show up in a PROC PRINT. It can also be used as a variable in the program. Just take care that you do not redefine the value in a way that inadvertently overrides the Do loop's incrementing.

The following is an example of using the index as a variable:

```
DO I = 1 to 10;
   Y = I * 10;
   PUT Y;
END;
```

This loop will multiply the numbers 1 to 10 by 10, producing the numbers 10 to 100, incremented each iteration by 10. It will output the results—10, 20, 30, 40, 50, 60, 70, 80, 90, 100—each on a separate line.

The SAS System increments the index each time the END is reached, then tests to see if it exceeded the rightmost value in the DO statement. When the value of the index is greater, execution "falls through" the loop and continues executing the following statements. If you output the value of the index (with a PUT or PROC PRINT), you will see that its value is 1 greater than the rightmost or terminal value. If you plan to use the index variable as a variable in the program, you must allow for this fact. If you assume that the index will represent the number of iterations of the loop, you will be off by 1.

DO UNTIL

The DO UNTIL statement creates a loop, but it iterates until a certain condition is met rather than iterating a set number of times. The statement must include the condition to be tested, as in

```
DO UNTIL (X = 3);
```

or

```
DO UNTIL (TOTAL > 10);
```

The condition specified on the DO UNTIL statement is tested at the end of the loop. If the condition is met or "true" when the END statement is executed, then execution will fall through the loop. Even if the condition is true at the time the loop is begun, the loop will be executed once, as in

```
X = 3;
DO UNTIL (X = 3);
    PUT 'This Will Be Output';
END;
```

In this case, X is equal to 3 when the DO UNTIL is executed, so the first itera-tion of the loop is carried out. When the condition on the DO UNTIL is tested at the end of the loop, it will be true, so execution will not return to the beginning of the loop. Instead, the program will continue after the END statement.

If the condition is not true at the beginning of the loop, and if it does not ever become true inside of the loop, then the loop will be endless, and execution will continue until execution is terminated from outside the SAS program. Consider the following example:

```
X = 3;
DO UNTIL (X = 4);
    PUT 'This Will Output Indefinitely';
END;
```

In this case, the loop will continue to iterate indefinitely, because there is no statement inside of the loop that will set X equal to 4. As long as X does not equal 4, the loop will continue to iterate. To solve this problem, you must put a statement inside the loop that will make X have the value of 4 and cause execu-tion to fall through the loop, as in

```
X = 3;
DO UNTIL (X = 4);
    PUT 'This Will Output and Stop';
    X = X + 1;
END;
```

In this case, the X = X + 1 will result in a value of 4 for X, which will be evalu-ated at the end of the first iteration. Thus, the loop will execute one time and fall through to the statements following the END.

You must be careful that you don't inadvertently write a program in which the test condition never becomes true. For example, if you initially set the condition on the DO UNTIL as true but change it inside the loop, the loop will be endless, as in the following:

```
X = 3;
DO UNTIL (X = 3);
   PUT 'This Will Not Stop';
   X = X + 1;
END;
```

In this case X was equal to 3 when the loop began; however, the X = X + 1 statement increments X before the loop ends. Thus, when the condition on the DO UNTIL is evaluated, it will not be true. Because X will continue to increment, it will never be equal to 3, and the loop will be endless. If this happens, you must terminate SAS manually. With the Windows version, you can do this by clicking on the X icon in the upper right-hand corner of the screen. You will get a dialog box that asks if you wish to terminate SAS or just the current program.

DO WHILE

The DO WHILE is the opposite of the DO UNTIL. The DO UNTIL statement iterates until a condition becomes true, whereas the DO WHILE iterates while a condition is true, or until a condition becomes false. You can accomplish most of the same tasks with either the DO WHILE or the DO UNTIL. The reason for the existence of both is that certain tasks are more easily accomplished with one or the other.

The form of the DO WHILE is similar to that of the DO UNTIL. You must specify the test condition on the statement, as in

```
DO WHILE (X = 3);
```
or
```
DO WHILE (N < 11);
```

Opposite to the DO UNTIL, the condition is tested at the beginning of the loop rather than at the end. This means that if the condition is true at the beginning of the loop, the statements in the loop will be executed. Execution will continue until the condition becomes false.

If the condition on the DO WHILE statement is initially not true, then the loop will not be executed at all, and execution will skip to the statements following the loop. Consider the following:

```
N = 10;
DO WHILE (N < 10);
  PUT 'This Will Not Be Output';
END;
```

In this case the loop will not be executed. Because N has a value of 10 when the DO WHILE is first executed, the condition N < 10 is not met. This is evaluated at the top of the loop, so the contents of the loop will be skipped.

As with the DO UNTIL, you must be careful not to inadvertently create an endless loop by failing to make the condition become false within the loop, as in

```
N = 1;
DO WHILE (N < 11);
  PUT 'This Will Output Indefinitely';
END;
```

N meets the condition of being less than 10 when the loop begins. Because it never changes its value within the loop, the loop is endless. To fix this problem, you might add a counter to increment N within the loop, as in

```
N = 1;
DO WHILE (N < 11);
  PUT 'This Will Not Output Indefinitely';
  N = N + 1;
END;
```

The counter N = N + 1 will allow for 10 iterations of the loop. At the beginning of the 11th iteration, N will be equal to 11, which makes the condition on the

DO WHILE false. Because N is no longer less than 11, execution will fall through the loop.

COIN FLIP SIMULATION
WITH A DO LOOP

An important use of computers in statistics is to conduct simulations or Monte Carlo studies. Monte Carlo studies are helpful to study empirically the behavior of statistical tests under known and controlled conditions. Random number generators allow you to draw samples of data from populations with known characteristics. Assumptions can be violated to determine the effects on the Type 1 or Type 2 error rates of a given statistic. A computer simulation program also can be used to model the outcomes of a probabilistic process, such as rolling dice or flipping a coin. Such simulations are useful as classroom demonstrations of sampling processes.

Program 6.1 is an example of a computer simulation program that models the flipping of a coin 100 times. It outputs the numbers of heads and tails. The uniform random number generator was used to "flip" the coin. This generator returns a random number between 0 and 1. To model the coin flip, you treat any number greater than .5 as a head and any number less than or equal to .5 as a tail. Thus, in theory half the observations will be heads and half will be tails. Of course, few samples of 100 coin flips will have exactly half heads and half tails.

Program 6.1 shows the SAS statements necessary to accomplish the simulation. Line 2 initializes three counters. NHEADS keeps track of the number of heads, NTAILS keeps track of the number of tails, and NTOT keeps track of the total number of flips. The Do loop is found in lines 3 to 8. Line 3 is a DO WHILE statement that says to repeat the loop until the variable NTOT, which is the total number of flips, reaches 100. Any number can be placed in the DO WHILE statement. To model 1,000 coin flips, 100 would be changed to 1,000. Line 4 draws a random number, which is evaluated in lines 5 and 6. Each of these two lines increments the head or tail counter depending on the value of the random number TOSS. Line 7 increments the number of flips by 1. Lines 9 to 11 output a report of the number of heads and tails.

Program 6.1

```
1    DATA FLIP;
2    NHEADS = 0; NTAILS = 0; NTOT = 0;
3    DO WHILE (NTOT < 100);
4        TOSS = RANUNI(-3);
5      IF TOSS > .5 THEN NHEADS = NHEADS + 1;
6      IF TOSS <= .5 THEN NTAILS = NTAILS + 1;
7        NTOT = NTOT + 1;
8    END;
9    FILE PRINT;
10   PUT 'Number of Heads = ' NHEADS;
11   PUT 'Number of Tails = ' NTAILS;
12   RUN;
```

The results of the program are in Output 6.1. In this case, there were 56 heads and 44 tails. The numbers of heads and tails may change each time the program is run.

NESTED LOOPS

So far, only individual loops have been considered. It is possible, however, to place loops within loops, creating what are called **nested loops**. Nested loops allow you to carry out procedures in a hierarchy. If a certain condition is met and then another is met, you carry out a procedure. This is not unlike a complex IF . . . THEN statement, where you specify that two conditions must be met with an AND. It is more flexible because you can execute statements between the

Output 6.1

```
The SAS System

Number of Heads = 56
Number of Tails = 44
```

two condition tests. Often the second condition is affected by statements that came after the first condition.

Consider the following statements:

```
DO I = 1 to 10;
  PUT 'This Prints For Each Iteration';
  DO WHILE (I = 10);
    PUT 'This Prints For The Last Iteration';
    STOP;
  END;
END;
```

The first or outer loop says to iterate 10 times. The PUT statement will be carried out each of the 10 times. The second or inner loop is executed only for the last case, when I equals 10. Its PUT statement will be carried out only once. Each DO must be ended with an END statement. The STOP statement is necessary in this particular program so that the inner loop will not be endless.

Note that indenting was used to make it easier to see the hierarchy or levels of loops. With several levels of nested loops, it becomes very difficult to match each DO to its END without indenting. Table 6.1 shows indenting with four levels of nested DOs. The indenting allows you to easily match each DO with its corresponding END because they will begin in the same column location. The outermost or first-level loop's DO and END are in the leftmost column. Among the inner loops, each level's DO and END are indented two spaces per level. The second level is indented two spaces, the third is indented four spaces, and so on. There are two loops at the third level in this example.

With nested loops that iterate, the innermost loop is completely executed (all iterations) for each iteration of the outer loop. You need to be careful about the level of the loops so that tasks are carried out in the order that you intend. With nested loops that use the DO Index=, you usually use different index values for the different nested loops. For example, you might use I for the inner loop and J for the outer loop. If you use the same index variable, the inner loop will reset the values of the outer loop index and not allow it to increment properly.

Program 6.2 illustrates how nested loops operate by outputting the values of the index variables from iteration to iteration of the program. This program will output 12 lines. The first time through the outer loop, J will have a value of 1. During each of the four iterations of the inner loop, J will continue to have a

Table 6.1
Indenting With Nested Do's

```
DO (First Level)
   .
   .
   .
   DO (Second Level)
      .
      .
      .
      DO (Third Level)
         .
         .
         .
         DO (Fourth Level)
            .
            .
            .
         END
      END
      DO (Third Level)
         .
         .
         .
      END
   END
END
```

value of 1. I will have the values from 1 to 4. During the second iteration of the outer loop, J will have a value of 2. When the inner loop is executed again, its index, I, will have values from 1 to 4. Finally, the third iteration of the outer loop will assign a value of 3 to J. The inner loop will iterate another four times, with I ranging from 1 to 4.

The results can be seen in Output 6.2. First J equals 1, and I increments from 1 to 4. Next, J equals 2, and I increments again from 1 to 4. Finally, J equals 3 and I increments from 1 to 4.

Program 6.2

```
1 DATA NESTED;
2 FILE PRINT;
3 DO J = 1 TO 3;
4   DO I = 1 TO 4;
5     PUT 'J = ' J @10 'I = ' I;
6   END;
7 END;
8 RUN;
```

SIMULATION OF THE VIOLATION OF *t*-TEST ASSUMPTIONS

Many examples of computer simulation or Monte Carlo studies to assess the impact of assumption violations can be found in the statistics literature. The computer is a powerful tool for determining how a statistic will behave when one or more of its assumptions are violated. As you will see below, such studies are not difficult to program, at least for simple statistics.

Program 6.3 is a simulation of the Type 1 error rate of an independent group *t* test when the assumption of homogeneity of variance is violated in the presence of unequal sample sizes. It is well known that the combination of larger variance with smaller sample size will disrupt the Type 1 error rate, and this program explores this property.

The Type 1 error rate is easy to assess because it involves calculating the proportion or percentage of significant *t*s when the underlying population means are the same. When assumptions are met, the proportion of significance should come close to the set significance level, which is normally .05.

This simulation makes use of the normal random number generator function to provide the observations to be analyzed. Observations are generated for each of two groups. To assess the Type 1 error rate, the means for both groups are set to the same value. At the $p < .05$ significance level, about 5% of the samples generated should yield statistically significant t tests. Deviation from 5% is indicative of a bias in the statistic.

The basic structure of a computer simulation program can be seen in the Figure 6.1 flowchart. The first step is to define the parameters for the problem.

Output 6.2

```
The SAS System

J = 1        I = 1
J = 1        I = 2
J = 1        I = 3
J = 1        I = 4
J = 2        I = 1
J = 2        I = 2
J = 2        I = 3
J = 2        I = 4
J = 3        I = 1
J = 3        I = 2
J = 3        I = 3
J = 3        I = 4
```

In this case, they include the significance level and, for each group, the population mean, population standard deviation, and sample size. The number of t tests to be computed is also specified. Specifying these parameters at the beginning of the program makes it easier to modify them on subsequent runs. The next three steps are placed inside a larger box in the flowchart to indicate that they represent a loop that iterates for each t test computed. Step 2 generates the data for each group, and Step 3 computes the t test. From iteration to iteration, the number of significant ts is counted in Step 4. Finally, Step 5 generates and outputs a report of the results.

Program 6.3 begins with a comment (lines 2-11) that defines the eight parameters that must be entered. The program allows you to specify the number of iterations at the beginning (line 13). It also allows you to enter the significance level (line 14), both population means (line 15), both population standard deviations (line 16), and both sample sizes (line 17). Line 20 initializes two accumulators. TOTT will accumulate the sum of the ts so that the mean t across iterations can be calculated. NSIG counts the number of significant t tests.

The next portion of program uses nested loops. The outermost loop, beginning at line 22, sets the number of iterations. The accumulators initialized in line 24 produce the necessary terms to calculate each t. The inner loop at lines 26 to 30 generates the data for the first group and accumulates the two necessary terms, which are the sum of the observations and the sum of the observations

Program 6.3

Simulation of Alpha Error Rates for *t* Test With Violation of Homogeneity of Variance and Equal Sample Size Assumptions

```
1   DATA TSIM;
2   **********************PARAMETERS******************
3   IT = number of iterations of the simulation.
4   PLEVEL = significance level for the t-tests.
5   MEANA = population mean for group A.
6   MEANB = population mean for group B.
7   SDA = population standard deviation for group A.
8   SDB = population standard deviation for group B.
9   NA = sample size for group A.
10  NB = sample size for group B.
11  *********************************************************;
12  *Set Parameters;
13  IT = 1000;
14  PLEVEL = .05;
15  MEANA = 100; MEANB = 100;
16  SDA = 10; SDB = 100;
17  NA = 20; NB = 5;
18  *Initialize accumulators for mean of ts and number
19  of significant ts;
20  TOTT = 0; NSIG = 0;
21  *Loop to determine number of iterations;
22  DO I = 1 TO IT;
23    *Initialize accumulators;
24    SUMXA = 0; SUMXB = 0; SUMXA2 = 0; SUMXB2 = 0;
25    *Generate and accumulate group A observations;
26    DO J = 1 TO NA;
27      XA = MEANA + SDA*RANNOR(0);
28      SUMXA = SUMXA + XA;
29      SUMXA2 = SUMXA2 + XA**2;
30    END;
31    *Generate and accumulate group B observations;
32    DO J = 1 TO NB;
33      XB = MEANB + SDB*RANNOR(0);
34      SUMXB = SUMXB + XB;
35      SUMXB2 = SUMXB2 + XB**2;
36    END;
37    *Compute t and its significance;
38    SSA = SUMXA2 - (SUMXA**2 / NA);
39    SSB = SUMXB2 - (SUMXB**2 / NB);
40    T = (SUMXA/NA - SUMXB/NB)/
```

(continued)

(continued)

```
41    SQRT((SSA+SSB)/(NA+NB-2)*(1/NA+1/NB));
42    DF = NA + NB - 2;
43    PT = 2 * PROBT((-1 * ABS(T)),DF);
44    *Accumulate ts and significances;
45    TOTT = TOTT + T;
46    IF PT < PLEVEL THEN NSIG = NSIG + 1;
47    END;
48 *Calculate mean t and percent significant;
49 MEANT = TOTT/IT;
50 PERCIG = 100 * NSIG / IT;
51 *Produce report of results;
52 FILE PRINT;
53 PUT @20 'Results of T-Test Simulation.' / /;
54 PUT @10 NSIG 'of ' IT '(' PERCIG
55 '%) t-tests were significant at p < ' PLEVEL;
56 PUT @10 'Mean value for t = ' MEANT;
57 PUT @10 'Means for the two groups = ' MEANA 'and ' MEANB;
58 PUT @10 'Standard deviations for the two groups = '
59 SDA 'and ' SDB;
60 PUT @10 'Sample sizes for the two groups = ' NA 'and ' NB;
61 RUN
```

squared. The inner loop at lines 32 to 36 does the same thing for the second group.

Lines 38 and 39 compute the sum of squares for each group. Lines 40 and 41 compute the t value, and line 42 computes the degrees of freedom. These t-test values are entered into the PROBT function (line 43) to yield the probability level for each t. Note that because the t value can be either positive or negative, the absolute value function (ABS) was used. To get the probability for the correct tail of the distribution, the t was then multiplied by -1. Line 45 accumulates the values of t to yield the sum of the t values across all iterations. Line 46 increments the counter by 1 if the t is significant for each iteration.

Once all iterations are completed, the program proceeds to produce a report (lines 52-60). An example is shown as Output 6.3. The program reports the number and percentage of significance ts. Note that it indicates what the set significance level was. In this case, the observed proportion of significance (.356) was far from the .05 that one would expect if assumptions were met. The mean value for t was also output, and it was $-.05109$ . . . for this example,

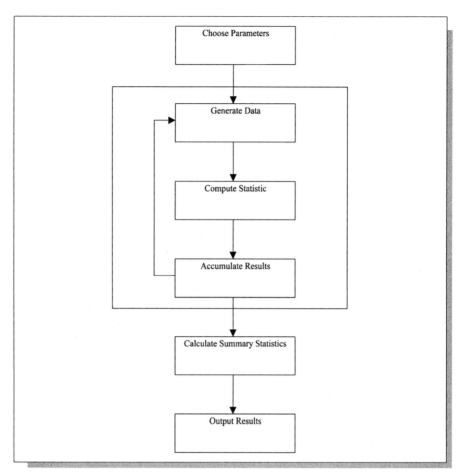

Figure 6.1. Flowchart for a Statistical Simulation Program

which is not very different from the expected mean of zero. The remainder of the report lists the other parameters that were set for this problem. Both population means, population standard deviations, and sample sizes were output.

The use of nested loops makes the logical flow of this program relatively simple and straightforward. The program can be used to test for other combinations of parameters just by modifying the values in lines 4 to 10. For example, if you set the sample sizes to be equal, you should find that the Type 1 error rate is approximately .05. You can also test the power of the statistic by making the population means unequal. The basic structure can be used to test the behavior of other statistics (e.g., analysis of variance) by modifying the program to generate the necessary data and compute the appropriate statistics.

COMMON ERRORS

One of the common errors with a Do loop is to forget the END statement, especially with nested loops. This will produce an error in the SAS Log telling you that the DO has no matching END. Indenting the loops as shown in the examples helps in keeping track of which statements are in which loops, as well as making it easier to keep the END statements in the correct place. A second error is putting the END statement in the wrong place and thereby either executing certain statements too many times or executing some statements too few times.

The DO UNTIL and DO WHILE statements have greater potential for error than the DO INDEX=. As noted earlier in the chapter, this is because it is an easy error to have the intended condition never occur with a DO UNTIL, or always occur with a DO WHILE. Both cases will produce an endless loop. If you encounter this situation, you can terminate the SAS program by clicking on the icon with an exclamation mark ("!") in a circle on the right of the menu bar near the top of the screen, or on the X icon in the upper right-hand corner. A likely error with the DO INDEX= is in having the limits as variables and having the values wrong. Thus, you might wish to have the loop run from 1 until the value of K, which you intend to be, say, 100 but actually is 1.

Another area that can cause a problem involves the index variables with nested loops. Always be sure to use different variable names for the indexes; otherwise, you might produce conflicts between the two loops, as in the following:

```
DO I = 1 TO 4;
  DO I = 1 TO 5;
    PUT I;
  END;
END;
```

This program will execute the inner loop only once, and I will be output only five times. When the inner loop has completed its first series of five iterations, the value of I will be 6, and thus the outer loop will not be executed a second

Output 6.3

```
The SAS System

                    Results of T-Test Simulation.

356 of 1000 (35.6%) t-tests were significant at p < 0.05
Mean value for t = -0.051092512
Means for the two groups = 100 and 100
Standard deviations for the two groups = 10 and 100
Sample sizes for the two groups = 20 and 5
```

time. If one of the index variable names is changed, say to J, the inner loop will execute four times and the value of I will be output 20 times.

⁓ Debugging Exercises ⁓

Exercise 6.1

```
    *Program to create table of squares of
numbers from 1 to 10;
    data squares;
    n = 1;
    file print;
    put "number" @25 "number squared";
    do while (n = 10);
      n = n + 1;
      n2 = n**2;
      put n @25 n2;
      end;
    run;
```

Exercise 6.2

This program is intended to compute sample means for four different populations with means 10, 25, 50, and 100. You should expect the computed sample means to be very close to these values—in most cases they will be within about 0.1 of the population values.

```
*Program to compute the mean of random
numbers where the population mean takes on
values of 10, 25, 50, 100;
data random;
sumx = 0;
n = 100;
file print;
do j = 10, 25, 50, 100; *Enter the popula-
tion values as constants;
   do j = 1 to n;
     x = rannor(-4) + j; *Generate
random numbers plus constants to create
population means;
     sumx = sumx + x;
   end;
meanx = sumx/n;
put "mean = " meanx;
end;
run;
```

Chapter 7

Arrays

A powerful programming feature of the SAS language is the ability to refer to two or more variables with a single variable name. Different variables given the same name are differentiated by number. If you had 10 variables, you could refer to them by the variable name X and distinguish them as X1, X2, X3, and so on to X10. For example, you might have data from a survey with 10 questions that would be assigned variables names survey1 to survey10. A group of variables sharing a name is termed an **array**. Arrays are used with Do loops to make manipulation of several variables much easier and more efficient. For example, suppose you have a psychological test with 100 items that were coded from 0 to 5, but the coding should have been from 1 to 6. You could add 1 to the value of each of the 100 variables by writing an expression for each, but it would take 100 expressions, as in

```
ITEM1 = ITEM1 + 1;
ITEM2 = ITEM2 + 1;
```

With an array and loop, three statements can add 1 to any number of variables that are part of the array, as in

```
DO I = 1 to 100;
  ITEM(I) = ITEM(I) + 1;
END;
```

To create an array, you must use the ARRAY statement to assign it a name, indicate how many variables or elements will be in it, and indicate the names of the variables in it. Individual array elements are referred to by number. Element numbers are assigned in the order in which variables are input into the array. Later in the program you can refer to individual elements of the array by the array name and element number.

ARRAY STATEMENT

The general form of the ARRAY statement is

```
ARRAY Name(size) variable list.
```

The following are valid ARRAY statements:

```
ARRAY X(10)  X1-X10;
ARRAY X(100) Y1-Y100;
ARRAY VAR(50)  X1-X10 Y1-Y40;
ARRAY VARS(5)  A B C D E;
```

In the first example, the array name is the same as the names of the variables that are assigned to it. In the second example, the array name is different from the names of the variables assigned to it. In the third example, the variables that are assigned to the array do not all have the same name. In fact, the variables assigned to an array do not have to be numbered, as in the fourth example.

ARRAY statements generally are placed near the beginning of a program, with the RETAIN, KEEP, and DROP statements. It is a good idea to place these definition-type statements that hold for the entire program in one place rather than scattering them throughout your program. In long programs, this will make them easier to find.

Individual elements of an array are referenced by their subscripts, placed in parentheses. Thus, the first element of an array named X would be X(1), the second element would be X(2), the third would be X(3), and so on. You can also refer to elements with variables as subscripts as in X(I) or X(J). The subscript variables must be whole numbers.

ONE-DIMENSIONAL ARRAYS

The simplest arrays are one dimensional. Think of a one-dimensional array as a single list of variables, much like a vector in matrix algebra. You can refer to an individual element of an array within a program by its array name followed by its subscript number in parentheses, such as X(2). The parentheses are necessary to refer to the array element. If the array X contains the element X2, then you can refer to X2 without the parentheses. This refers to the original variable, however, and not the array element.

In most programs, it is rare to refer to an individual element by number. Usually a more general designation is used, such as X(I) or Y(J). Values of I and J are set by the program. To refer to X(2), you would first set the index variable I to the value of 2, then use X(I) in a statement, as in

```
I = 2;
PUT X(I);
```

These two statements will result in the outputting of X(2).

Arrays are mainly used within Do Index= loops, where the index is used to refer to the various elements within the array. The Do loops discussed in Chapter 6 began with 1 and were incremented by 1. DO statements are more flexible and allow you to increment by numbers other than 1 and to list specific elements.

To change the increment, you must add a BY and increment number to the DO statement, as in

```
DO I = 1 TO 10 BY 2.
```

This statement will begin by setting I equal to 1 and then increment I by 2, so that it will take on the values 1, 3, 5, 7, and 9. It is also possible for the loop to increment in the opposite direction, beginning with the largest number and incrementing downward, as in

```
DO I = 10 TO 1 BY -1.
```

In this case, the first number immediately following the equal sign is the largest. The number following the TO is the smallest. The negative sign on the increment following the BY says to decrease I each iteration by 1. It is possible to use other negative whole numbers.

Another option with a DO statement is to list the individual values for the index variable, following the equal sign. The following are examples:

```
DO I = 1, 2, 3, 4, 5;
DO J = 1, 3, 4, 7, 8, 10;
DO INDEXN = 4, 7, 8, 12, 22;
```

In each of these cases, the index variable will take on only the values in the list, beginning with the leftmost and proceeding one by one until the last one. The first case will iterate five times, the second will iterate six times, and the third case will iterate five times.

SCORING PSYCHOLOGICAL TESTS WITH ARRAYS

A task frequently done by social scientists is the combining of individual items of a psychological test or scale into total scores. A similar task might be done where multiple observations of some phenomenon are combined into totals, such as monthly inflation rates combined into annual rates, or statewide poll results combined into nationwide results.

With a psychological test, the various items are summed into a total score, which is a quite simple task. There are two aspects, however, that make the process somewhat more complex. First, items are not always scored in the same direction. Sometimes a high score on an item represents a high value on the underlying construct of interest, and sometimes a high score on an item represents a low value on the underlying construct. If the test is designed to assess attitudes toward computers, the item "I love computers" would be scored in one direction, whereas the item "I hate computers" would be scored in the opposite direction. Items are usually quantified by numbering the response choices from 1 to the number of choices, for example 1 to 5. Items that are scaled in the reverse direction have their choices numbered in reverse order, for example 5 to 1. A simple trick to reverse the scoring for an item is to add the highest possible number to the lowest (e.g., $1 + 5$ in the present example) and subtract each item to be reversed from this number. Thus, a 1 becomes a 5 ($6 - 1 = 5$), a 2 becomes a 4 ($6 - 2 = 4$), a 3 stays a 3 ($6 - 3 = 3$), a 4 becomes a 2 (6 − 4 = 2), and a 5 becomes a 1 (6 − 5 = 1). (See Spector, 1992, for additional discussion of scoring.)

The other problem is that sometimes respondents fail to complete all items. You usually don't throw out an entire case because of a missing item or two. One way to handle the problem is to compute a score based on the available items, then substitute the respondent's mean response for the missing items. Of course, if most of the items are missing, you would want to delete the respondent's score.

Program 7.1 is an example of scoring some hypothetical psychological tests. Twenty items for eight cases were input as shown in Table 7.1. There were missing data for some items for cases 4, 5, and 8. The first 10 items had response choices that ranged from 1 to 5, and the second 10 items had response choices that ranged from 1 to 7. These items were combined into three separate scores.

Table 7.2 shows the major steps involved in the scoring program. First, the items are input and placed into an array. The use of an array inside of a Do loop will make the programming task easier. The second step is to reverse score the negatively worded items. Third, the missing items are converted from the SAS missing value designation "." to zero. This is necessary because the value of an expression is set equal to missing when the value of a variable on the right-hand side of the expression is missing. Setting the missing values equal to zero will allow the sum of nonmissing items to be accumulated. The fourth step is to sum the items for each subscale and to count the number of nonmissing items. Fifth, the total scores are adjusted for the missing items by substituting the mean response for the missing items. To accomplish this, the total score is divided by the number of nonmissing items and then multiplied by the total number of items in the scale. For example, suppose a four-item scale has three nonmissing items with values 2, 3, and 4. Their sum will be 9, and their mean will be 3. If you were to substitute the mean, 3, for the missing item, you would have a total score of 12. Multiplying the mean, 3, by the total number of items, 4, also yields the total score of 12. The sixth step is to round the scores to one digit to the right of the decimal. Next, scale scores based on too many missing values are eliminated, and finally the individual scores for each case are output.

The program itself begins with a brief message explaining what the program was designed to accomplish (lines 1-4). The data were input from an external file, named score.dat. Each case included a case number, named ID,

Table 7.1

Input Data for Program 7.1

```
0115342415241243276775
0251514233527767511243
0333332424247665632322
041 3 1 254576 532112
0515    2 33765
0613234353335554565565
0715253424331212566765
08 152515243534 7765
```

and the 20 items (see line 7). The items were all placed into an array (line 8) named X.

The loop at lines 11 to 13 reverse scores items 1, 3, 5, 7, and 9. Because they had a five-point scale that ranged from 1 to 5, each item was subtracted from 6. The loop at lines 14 to 16 reverse scores items 11, 12, 13, and 15. These items had a seven-point scale that ranged from 1 to 7, so each was subtracted from 8. The loop at lines 18 to 20 converts the missing values (to which the SAS System assigns a value of ".") to 0.

Table 7.2

Step-by-Step Procedure for Program 7.1

1. Input items into an array
2. Reverse score items
3. Convert missing items to zeros
4. Sum items and count nonmissing items
5. Compute total scores adjusted for missing items
6. Round scores
7. Eliminate scores with too many missing values
8. Output scores

Program 7.1
Program to Score and Analyze Psychological Test Data

```
1    *Program to score a psychological test. Data are entered
2    from an external data file. Program reverses the scoring
3    of reverse keyed items. Program allows for missing data
4    by substituting mean of existing items for missing items;
5    DATA SCORE;
6      INFILE 'score.dat';
7      INPUT ID 2. (ITEM1-ITEM20) (1.);
8      ARRAY X(20) ITEM1-ITEM20;
9      KEEP SCALE1-SCALE3;
10     *Reverse score items;
11     DO I = 1, 3, 5, 7, 9;
12       X(I) = 6 - X(I);
13     END;
14     DO I = 11, 12, 13, 15;
15       X(I) = 8 - X(I);
16     END;
17     *Convert missing values to 0;
18     DO I = 1 TO 20;
19       IF X(I) = . THEN X(I) = 0;
20     END;
21     *Initialize item counters;
22     K1 = 0; K2 = 0; K3 = 0;
23     *Initialize score accumulators;
24     SCALE1 = 0; SCALE2 = 0; SCALE3 = 0;
25     *Sum items in each subscale;
26     DO I = 1 TO 10;
27       SCALE1 = SCALE1 + X(I);
28       IF X(I) > 0 THEN K1 = K1 + 1;
29     END;
30     DO I = 11, 13, 19, 20;
31       SCALE2 = SCALE2 + X(I);
32       IF X(I) > 0 THEN K2 = K2 + 1;
33     END;
34     DO I = 12, 14, 15, 16, 17, 18;
35       SCALE3 = SCALE3 + X(I);
36       IF X(I) > 0 THEN K3 = K3 + 1;
37     END;
38     *Adjust total scores for missing items;
39     SCALE1 = SCALE1/K1*10;
40     SCALE2 = SCALE2/K2*4;
41     SCALE3 = SCALE3/K3*6;
42     *Round scores;
43     SCALE1 = ROUND(SCALE1,.1);
44     SCALE2 = ROUND(SCALE2,.1);
45     SCALE3 = ROUND(SCALE3,.1);
46     *Eliminate scores based on half the items or fewer;
```

(continued)

(continued)

```
47    IF K1 < 6 THEN SCALE1 = .;
48    IF K2 < 3 THEN SCALE2 = .;
49    IF K3 < 4 THEN SCALE3 = .;
50 PROC PRINT;
51 RUN;
```

The next section of the program computes the scale scores for each of the three scales. It also computes the number of nonmissing items for each scale. The item counters are initialized to zero in line 22. The scale accumulators are initialized to zero in line 24. The following three Do loops compute the sum of the items and count the number of nonmissing items for the three scales. As you can see in lines 28, 32, and 36, the counters are incremented by one for each item that is greater than zero. Because only missing values are equal to zero, items with values greater than zero are nonmissing.

The expressions in lines 39 to 41 adjust each score for the number of items. Dividing each item sum by its number of nonmissing items yields the mean score per item. Multiplying the mean by the total number of items in the scale yields a score that is equivalent to substituting the mean score for the nonzero items for the missing item.

The three scale scores are rounded by the statements in lines 43 to 45. This is necessary because the missing values adjustment sometimes results in total scores that have several digits to the right of the decimal. Lines 47 to 49 set the values of the scale scores equal to zero if too many of the items are missing. In this case, there must be more than half the items present to keep the score for a case.

A PROC PRINT was used to print the three scores for each case. The results can be seen in Output 7.1. As you can see, all three scale scores for cases 1, 2, 3, and 6 were whole numbers. These four cases had no missing data, so the total contains no fractions. Cases 4 and 7 had some missing data, and this is reflected in the totals, which were not whole numbers. Note, however, that it is possible even with missing items to have a whole number total. Case 5 has missing values for the Scale 1 and Scale 2 totals. This is because there were half or more missing items for these scales. In fact, as can be seen in Table 7.1, only one of five items were nonmissing for each of these scales.

Output 7.1

```
The SAS System

        OBS    SCALE1   SCALE2   SCALE3
          1     43.0     23.0     35.0
          2     17.0     10.0     15.0
          3     36.0      7.0     17.0
          4     41.4      5.3     13.2
          5       .        .      32.0
          6     40.0     25.0     30.0
          7     46.3     21.0     31.5
```

MULTIDIMENSIONAL ARRAYS

Arrays can be organized into any number of multiple dimensions. Most multi-dimensional arrays have two dimensions, which enables them to represent matrices. This allows for easy programming of matrix algebra procedures, which represent highly efficient approaches to many statistical and data analytic problems.

A **matrix** is a two-dimensional array of elements (numbers, characters, or variables) arranged in rows and columns. The smallest matrix possible has four elements arranged in two rows and two columns. Table 7.3 shows a 2 × 2 (read "2 by 2") matrix. The elements can be referred to by their row and column numbers, with the row listed first. Hence, the value of 1 in the table is the 1,1 element, 2 is the 2,1 element, 3 is the 1,2 element, and 4 is the 2,2 element. Matrices can be larger than 2 × 2 and can be of any size.

A multidimensional array differs from a one-dimensional array only in that the size of the array has multiple numbers representing the different dimensions. Examples are

```
ARRAY (2,2) X1-X4;
ARRAY (3,2) X1-X6;
ARRAY (2,3,2) X1-X12;
```

The first case reads in a 2 × 2 matrix, where the first 2 represents rows and the second 2 represents columns. The X variables are read into rows of the array, so that X1 is the 1,1 element, X2 is the 1,2 element, X3 is the 2,1 element, and X4 is the 2,2 element. It is important to be careful to refer to the elements in the correct order.

The second case has three rows and two columns. Arrays do not have to have the same number of rows and columns. The third case has three dimensions. You refer to each element by its three-dimensional designations. The dimensions are incremented from right to left. X1 is the 1,1,1 element, X2 is the 1,1,2 element, X3 is the 1,2,1 element, X4 is the 1,2,2 element, and so on. The entire sequence is shown in Table 7.4.

The manipulation of multidimensional arrays within a program requires juggling multiple subscripts. This involves the use of nested Do loops, one for each dimension of the array. Each loop uses a different variable name for its index, and the index variables match the subscript variables in the array. Take, for example, the problem of adding 1 to each element in a 3×4 array, created with

```
ARRAY Y(3,4) Y1-Y12;
```

To add 1 to each element, or Y(I,J), you must create the appropriate expression:

```
Y(I,J) = Y(I,J) + 1;
```

By using the variables I and J in the expression, you can refer to individual elements in the array by assigning values to I and J. To do this efficiently, you can embed the expression in two nested loops, as

```
DO I = 1 TO 3;
  DO J = 1 TO 4;
    Y(I,J) = Y(I,J) + 1;
  END;
END;
```

As discussed previously, the nested loops begin with both I and J equal to 1. The inner loop will iterate J from 1 to 4. Then I will be incremented to 2, and J will iterate from 1 to 4. Finally, I will be incremented to 3, and J will iterate from 1 to 4. All 12 possible combinations of I and J will occur. The expression will replace each of the values in Y(I,J) with the original value plus 1.

Care must be taken with these arrays so that you don't refer to an element that does not exist. In the above example, if you had reversed the I and J in the

Table 7.3

2 × 2 Matrix

$$\begin{pmatrix} 1 & 2 \\ 3 & 4 \end{pmatrix}$$

loops, you would have assigned a value to 1 of 4, which is beyond the range of the array, because it has only three rows. You will get a "subscript out of range" error in your SAS Log if this occurs.

Table 7.4

Variable Name	Array Element
X1	1,1,1
X2	1,1,2
X3	1,2,1
X4	1,2,2
X5	1,3,1
X6	1,3,2
X7	2,1,1
X8	2,1,2
X9	2,2,1
X10	2,2,2
X11	2,3,1
X12	2,3,2

HANDLING TWO-DIMENSIONAL DATA USING MULTIDIMENSIONAL ARRAYS

It is common to have multiple observations that are organized into a factorial structure. For example, one might have job performance data on a group of subjects where there are multiple dimensions of performance (e.g., work quality, work quantity, and attendance) and multiple raters (different people) of performance. The factorial structure arises when each rater provides a measure of each performance dimension. With such data, one might wish to sum across all raters for each dimension to yield dimension scores. Alternately, one might wish to sum across all dimensions to get rater scores.

One way to handle such data is to place them in a matrix in which rows represent dimensions and columns represent raters. Summing across rows will yield rater scores, and summing across columns will yield dimension scores.

Program 7.2 illustrates how this is done using multidimensional arrays with nested Do loops. The program enters a 4 × 5 matrix of numbers that represents rater by dimension data. It then sums and prints rater totals and dimension totals by summing each row of the matrix and each column of the matrix, respectively. As you can see in the data line following the DATALINES statement, each row of the matrix contains the integers from 1 to 5. Each row total equals 15 (the sum of the numbers 1 to 5). The column totals are 4, 8, 12, 16, and 20 (1 × 4, 2 × 4, 3 × 4, 4 × 4, and 5 × 4).

The program inputs (line 2) 20 variables named X1 to X20. Line 3 organizes the 20 variables into a 4 × 5 array named X. Line 4 creates a one-dimensional array (RTOT) that will hold the four row totals (ROW1 to ROW4), and line 5 creates a one-dimensional array (CTOT) that will hold the five column totals (COL1 to COL5). Note that these variables have not been input but are created within the program itself.

The first two loops encountered in the program (lines 6 to 8 and lines 9 to 11) initialize the elements of RTOT and CTOT to equal zero. If you don't initialize them, they will have missing values initially, and you will not be able to use them as accumulators later on.

Lines 12 to 16 contain two nested loops that calculate the row totals. In line 14, where the summing is accomplished, I represents rows and J represents columns. Because the inner loop increments J or the columns at each level of I or rows, this nested pair of loops processes the elements across rows. Table 7.5 shows the order of processing. First, the outer loop is set to the first row, or I = 1, and the inner loop adds the five column elements of the first row, or J = 1

Program 7.2

```
1   DATA RATERS;
2     INPUT (X1-X20) (1.);
3     ARRAY X(4,5) X1-X20;
4     ARRAY RTOT(4) ROW1-ROW4;
5     ARRAY CTOT(5) COL1-COL5;
6     DO I = 1 TO 4;  *Initialize row accumulators;
7       RTOT(I) = 0;
8     END;
9     DO I = 1 TO 5;  *Initialize column accumulators;
10    CTOT(I) = 0;
11    END;
12    DO I = 1 TO 4;   *Compute row totals;
13      DO J = 1 TO 5;
14        RTOT(I) = RTOT(I) + X(I,J);
15      END;
16    END;
17    FILE PRINT;
18    PUT 'RATER TOTALS' /;
19    DO I = 1 TO 4;   *Print row totals;
20      PUT 'Rater 'I'= ' RTOT(I);
21    END;
22    DO I = 1 TO 4;   *Compute column totals;
23      DO J = 1 TO 5;
24        CTOT(J) = CTOT(J) + X(I,J);
25      END;
26    END;
27    FILE PRINT;
28    PUT / 'DIMENSION TOTALS' /;
29    DO I = 1 TO 5;   *Print column totals;
30      PUT 'Dimension ' I '= ' CTOT(I);
31    END;
32 DATALINES;
12345123451234512345
;
RUN;
```

to 5. The RTOT array is subscripted by I so that all five elements for each row are added to the corresponding row total. In other words, first the five elements

Table 7.5
Order of Processing for Nested Loops in Example 7.2

	Column 1	Column 2	Column 3	Column 4	Column 5
Row 1	1	2	3	4	5
Row 2	6	7	8	9	10
Row 3	11	12	13	14	15
Row 4	16	17	18	19	20

for row 1 are summed and put into RTOT(1), then the five elements for row 2, and so on until all four rows have been summed. The loop at lines 19 to 21 outputs the four row totals, as you can see in Output 7.2.

The nested loops in lines 22 to 26 calculate the column totals. The only difference between this part of the program and the part that computed the row totals is the subscript on the CTOT array. In this case it is J, which represents the column instead of I, which now represents the row. The individual elements of X are summed in the same order as before, but they don't go into the same accumulators. Rather, on each iteration of the outer loop, the inner loop places one element in each of the five column totals. This procedure iterates until all five elements for each column have been summed. Thus, rather than producing a total at each iteration of the outer loop, all final totals are produced at the last iteration of the outer loop. The column totals are output by the loop at lines 29 to 31. The resulting output can be seen in Output 7.2.

PROGRAMMING MATRIX
ALGEBRA OPERATIONS

SAS arrays and loops make it possible to program matrix algebra operations quite easily. These operations are very useful for certain types of problems because they allow for general solutions. General solutions minimize the modifications you must make to run problems of different sizes. This section will show

Output 7.2

```
RATER TOTALS

Rater 1 = 15
Rater 2 = 15
Rater 3 = 15
Rater 4 = 15

DIMENSION TOTALS

Dimension 1 = 4
Dimension 2 = 8
Dimension 3 = 12
Dimension 4 = 16
Dimension 5 = 20
```

you how to write a program to compute a sum of squares and cross-products (SSCP) matrix from deviation scores. The SSCP matrix contains the sums of squares and cross-products for two or more variables. The main diagonal elements of the matrix contain the sums of squares, and the off-diagonal elements contain the sums of cross-products. If you divide the SSCP elements by the sample size, you convert the matrix to a variance-covariance matrix. (For additional discussion of SSCP matrices, see Namboodiri, 1984.)

To compute the SSCP matrix, you begin with a data matrix of deviation scores. In the data matrix, each row represents an individual case and each column represents a variable. A deviation score is the raw score minus its mean. For a given sample, you compute the mean across cases for each variable and subtract the mean from each raw score. For Program 7.3, a data matrix of deviation scores was created that represents five cases assessed on three variables (see Table 7.6).

Computing the SSCP matrix from a data matrix involves two matrix operations. First, the data matrix is transposed, and second, the transposed matrix is multiplied by the original data matrix. The resulting matrix is the SSCP matrix, which is, in algebraic terms

```
SSCP = XΨX<
```

Table 7.6
Data Matrix for Program 7.3

	Variable 1	Variable 2	Variable 3
Case 1	-2	-2	3
Case 2	-1	-2	-1
Case 3	0	1	1
Case 4	1	0	-2
Case 5	2	3	-1

where X is the data matrix.

Before proceeding to the program itself, the two operations will be reviewed briefly. If the explanation is insufficient, you might wish to consult a text on matrix algebra, such as Namboodiri (1984). Additional operations can be programmed by extending the principles outlined here.

Matrix Transpose

The *matrix transpose* reverses the rows and columns of a matrix. Thus, the first row becomes the first column, the second row becomes the second column, and so on. In the transposed data matrix, the rows represent the variables and the columns represent the cases. Table 7.7 shows an example of a matrix and its transpose. As can be seen, the first row containing the elements 1, 2, and 3 became the first column, and the second row containing the elements 4, 5, and 6 became the second column.

Matrix Multiplication

Matrix multiplication is a more complex operation than the transpose. It involves taking two matrices and completing an operation involving each row

---

Table 7.7

Example of a Matrix, Its Transpose, and the Product of the Two

$$X = \begin{pmatrix} 1\ 2\ 3 \\ 4\ 5\ 6 \end{pmatrix} \qquad X' = \begin{pmatrix} 1\ 4 \\ 2\ 5 \\ 3\ 6 \end{pmatrix} \qquad XX' = \begin{pmatrix} 14\ 32 \\ 32\ 77 \end{pmatrix}$$

---

of the leftmost matrix with each column of the rightmost matrix. For each row and column pair, you match up the corresponding elements (i.e., first element of the row with first element of the column, second element of the row with second element of the column, etc.). The matched elements are multiplied together, and the products are summed. The row and column numbers represent the row by column designation for the resultant matrix. Take the two matrices in Table 7.7. The first row of X consists of a 1, 2, and 3. The first column of $X\Psi$ also consists of a 1, 2, and 3. You multiply 1×1, 2×2, and 3×3, yielding 1, 4, and 9. You then add them up, yielding a sum of 14 (see Table 7.7). This is the 1, 1 element of the resultant matrix because it involved row 1 of the leftmost matrix and column 1 of the rightmost matrix. You repeat the operation for the first row and second column, which yields a total of 32 ($1 \times 4 + 2 \times 5 + 3 \times 6$). Next you match the second row of X with both columns of $X\Psi$. The second row versus first column yields a total of 32 (4 1 + 5 2 + 6 3). The second row with the second columns yields a 77 (4 4 + 5 5 + 6 6). Note that the matrix is symmetrical (i.e., the 1,2 element and 2,1 element on either side of the main diagonal are equal, in this case 32). Also note that the diagonal elements are the sum of the squared elements of each row of the leftmost matrix.

The SSCP Matrix Program

The basic structure of Program 7.3 to compute the SSCP matrix is not much different from the structure of Program 7.2. The data are read into a matrix, although in this case the matrix has two dimensions. A series of Do loops is used first to transpose the data matrix, then multiply the transpose by the original. Finally, the resultant matrix is output.

Lines 1 to 3 begin the data step, input the data matrix, and place it in Array X. Array XT (line 4) will contain the transpose of array X. Array SS (line 5) will contain the SSCP matrix. Lines 7 to 11 create the elements of Array XT, which is the transpose of Array X. Because the array has two dimensions, two nested loops are necessary to operate on each element of Array X. The transformation itself is accomplished by making every I,J element of Array XT equal to every J,I element of Array X. Thus, element 1,2 becomes element 2,1, element 1,3 becomes element 3,1, and so on.

The lines from 13 to 25 accomplish the multiplication. Because the multiplication operation involves accumulating sums, you have to initialize the elements of Array SS. This is done by the nested loops in lines 13 to 17. Because Array SS is two dimensional, you need the nested loops with different indices (I and J) to cover all elements. Line 15 sets them to 0.

The multiplication itself is done by the three nested loops in lines 19 to 25. These loops are at three levels, each with a different index, I, J, and K. This is necessary because the operation requires you to choose a row from Array XT and a column from Array X, then operate across the row and down the column. The outermost loop works on the rows of Array XT one by one. The second level loop works on each column of Array X, once the outer loop has chosen a row of Array XT. Thus, row 1 of Array XT is processed with columns 1, 2, 3, 4, and then 5 of Array X. Then row 2 of Array XT is processed with columns 1 to 5 of Array X. Finally, row 3 of Array XT is processed with columns 1 to 5 of Array X.

Once the outer and middle loops have selected a row and column to process, the multiplications and summations must be done. The corresponding row element of Array XT is matched to the corresponding column element of Array X. Take the first row of Array XT and the first column of Array X. XT(1,1) is matched to X(1,1), XT(1,2) is matched to X(2,1), XT(1,3) is matched to X(3,1), and so on. Note that the row subscript of Array XT remains constant and the column subscript of Array X remains constant. The column subscript of Array XT and the row subscript of Array X match each other across the pairs, and they increment from 1 to 3.

Now analyze what is happening in line 22. Array SS will contain the final matrix, so it is subscripted by I and J, representing the rows and columns. It is also an accumulator, which sums the products that go into each element of Array SS. Array XT has the subscript I for its rows and K for its columns. Array X

Program 7.3

```
1   DATA SSCP;
2     INPUT (X1-X15) (2.);
3     ARRAY X(5,3) X1-X15;
4     ARRAY XT(3,5) XT1-XT15;
5     ARRAY SS(3,3) SS1-SS9;
6     *Transpose data matrix X;
7     DO I = 1 TO 3;
8       DO J = 1 TO 5;
9         XT(I,J) = X(J,I);
10      END;
11    END;
12    *Initialize accumulators for SSCP elements;
13    DO I = 1 TO 3;
14      DO J = 1 TO 3;
15        SS(I,J) = 0;
16      END;
17    END;
18    *Premultiply X by XT;
19    DO I = 1 TO 3;
20      DO J = 1 TO 3;
21        DO K = 1 TO 5;
22        SS(I,J) = SS(I,J) + (XT(I,K) * X(K,J));
23        END;
24      END;
25    END;
26    FILE PRINT;
27  PUT 'SUM OF SQUARES AND CROSS-PRODUCTS MATRIX'
/;
28    DO I = 1 TO 3;
29      PUT @3 @;
30      DO J = 1 TO 3;
31        PUT SS(I,J) @;
32      END;
33      PUT;
34    END;
35 DATALINES;
-2-2 3-1-2-1 0 1 1 1 0-2 2 3-1
;
RUN;
```

Output 7.3

```
The SAS System

SUM OF SQUARES AND CROSS-PRODUCTS MATRIX

    10  12  -9
    12  18  -6
    -9  -6  16
```

has the subscript K for its rows and J for its columns. Given a row and column pair to process, the innermost loop will use the K subscript to iterate through the three pairs of corresponding elements to multiply.

This can be seen more easily if you mentally execute an iteration of the first two loops. First set I to 1 and J to 1, meaning that you will be matching the first row of Array XT to the first column of Array X to yield the SS(1,1) element. K is initially equal to 1. Looking at line 22 from right to left, multiply XT(1,1) by X(1,1), or -2×-2, and add the result to SS(1,1), which was initialized to 0. Increment K to 2 and multiply XT(1,2) by X(2,1) or -1×-1, and add it to SS(1,1), which this time was equal to 4. Increment K to 3 and multiply XT(1,3) by X(3,1) or 0×0, and add it to SS(1,1). This continues through the five pairs of elements in the first row of Array XT and first column of Array X. Next, the middle loop is incremented to 2, and the same procedure is repeated to calculate SS(1,2).

When processing of these nested loops is complete, Array SS will be the product of the two matrices. The resulting SSCP matrix can be seen in Output 7.3.

COMMON ERRORS

A frequent error with an array when used in a loop is to refer to a nonexistent array variable. For example, suppose you define an array to have 10 variables, but in your loop you increment it 11 times, say from 1 to 11. Because the 11th variable does not exist in the array, you will get an error in the SAS Log "Array subscript out of range."

Another potential trouble spot concerns the correspondence between the index variable in the loop and the index for the array. It is easy to mix them up and refer to the wrong array element. This is particularly true when you are using nested loops, or when you have multidimensional arrays. A great deal of testing is required to be sure you have not mixed up indices.

⌇ *Debugging Exercises* ⌇

Exercise 7.1

```
*Program to add 1 to each item of a psychological test;
data scale;
input (x1-x10)(1.);
array x(10) x1-x10;
do i = 1 to 12;
  x = x + 1;
end;
datalines;
0123401234
1111155555
;
proc print;
run;
```

Exercise 7.2

This exercise does matrix addition on two 2 × 4 matrices, A and B. This operation involves summing corresponding elements of the two matrices. It should produce a 2 × 4 matrix as follows:

$$\begin{pmatrix} 5 & 6 & 6 & 7 \\ 7 & 8 & 8 & 9 \end{pmatrix}$$

```
*Program to add two matrices, A and B;
data MatrixAddition;
input (a1-a8)(1.) / (b1-b8)(1.);
array a(2,4) a1-a8;
array b(2,4) b1-b8;
array both(2,4) both1-both8;
file print;
do j = 1 to 2;
  do i = 1 to 4;
    both(i,j) = a(i,j) + b(i,j);
    put both(i,j);
  end;
  put;
end;
datalines;
11223344
45454545
run;
```

Manipulating Files

So far the discussion of inputting and outputting has involved one file at a time. Some earlier program examples had multiple data steps within a program, but the manipulation of multiple data files has been limited. This chapter will discuss how you can handle several files at one time. This can involve the inputting of two or more files into a single data step, or outputting from a data step into two or more files. In addition, there will be further discussion of manipulating single files. This might involve moving a file from one location to another, or modifying a file.

INPUTTING MULTIPLE FILES

Multiple files can be put together into a single SAS data set. There are two ways in which multiple files can be combined. Concatenation involves adding the cases from one file to the cases of another. In most instances of concatenation, both original files contain cases that share the same variables, although there can be variables in one file that are not in the other. Concatenation can be thought of as a vertical combination of files in that it makes the file longer by adding more cases. It does not make it wider, in that data from both files are not combined in a way that makes the cases longer. Figure 8.1 illustrates concatenation. As it shows, the combined file is longer vertically than either of its subfiles, but they are both of the same horizontal width. This is also illustrated in Table 8.1. Assume we have three files, A, B, and C. All three have as the first variable the subject two-digit ID. Files A and C also contain a variable for gender, whereas File B contains a variable for age. The concatenation example shows that the cases for File C are added to the bottom of File A. The resulting file has more cases than the original files but the same number of variables.

Merging, on the other hand, is when two or more files have different variables from the same cases. In many instances, every case is represented in each file, but this is not necessary for merging to occur. For the most part, merging does not result in a longer file; rather, it results in a file that has longer cases. As can be seen in Figure 8.1, merging combines files horizontally. Table 8.1 shows how Files A and B are merged. The resulting file has the ID and gender variables in the same place as the original File A, and the age variable added to the right for each case. The number of cases is the same as in the original files, but the file has more variables.

Concatenation

To concatenate files, they must be in SAS data sets—either within a permanent SAS data library or as SAS working data sets. Take the case in which you wish to concatenate two data sets that are both in non-SAS data files. You would create two data steps, one to input the first file, say DATA A, and the other to input the second file, say DATA B. You would then create a third data step that would use a set statement to list the two data sets to concatenate, as in

```
DATA BOTH;
SET A B;
```

These two statements will instruct the computer to create a SAS data set named BOTH that contains data set B added to the end of data set A. Following statements can then manipulate the data from the combined or concatenated data set.

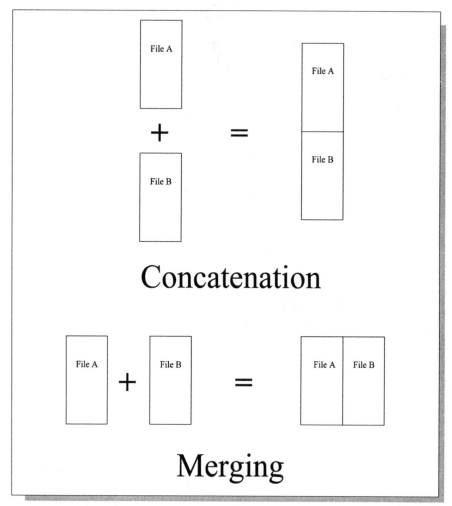

Figure 8.1. Illustration of File Concatenation and File Merging

Merging

Merging is accomplished by means of a MERGE statement. Here again, the data sets to be merged must be SAS data sets. Just as with the SET statement, you list the files to be combined on the MERGE statement, as in

Table 8.1

File A	File B	File C
01 m	01 19	05 m
02 m	02 22	06 m
03 f	03 23	07 f
04 f	04 18	08 f

Merging of File A and File B

```
01 m 19
02 m 22
03 f 23
04 f 18
```

Concatenation of File A and File C

```
01 m
02 m
03 f
04 f
05 m
06 m
07 f
08 f
```

```
MERGE A B;
```

Because merging involves the matching of corresponding cases, you must indicate how the matching is to be done. If you use the MERGE statement alone, the computer will match all the first cases in each file together, all the second cases in each file together, all the third cases in each file together, and so on.

This works fine as long as every file contains every case, and the cases are in the same order in each file. One misplaced case can upset the order and result in mismatched cases.

A safer way to match the cases is to provide a unique case or identifying number for each case in each file. You must be certain that corresponding cases across files share the same identifying number, such as an assigned case number or a social security number. You can instruct the computer to match on the case number with a BY statement, as in

```
MERGE A B; BY ID;
```

or

```
MERGE FIRST SECOND; BY SOCSEC;
```

In order to use a BY statement, every file being merged must be sorted by the variable on the BY. If any one of the files is not sorted, you will get an error message in the SAS Log, instructing you to sort. Sorting can be done with PROC SORT, which is discussed in the following section.

Before you can merge data sets, you must set up a data step to name the resulting merged data set. Thus, a MERGE statement will be preceded by a DATA statement, as in

```
DATA BOTH;
MERGE ONE TWO; BY ID;
```

The data sets ONE and TWO must have been created earlier in the program or be in a SAS data library, as in

```
DATA COMBINE;
MERGE SASUSER.ONE SASUSER.TWO; BY CASEN;
```

The two files must have been sorted by ID in the first example and CASEN in the second. If the data sets happen to have been sorted appropriately before input, PROC SORT does not have to be run.

SORTING WITH PROC SORT

File sorting can be done with PROC SORT. This procedure allows you to sort a file in ascending or descending order according to a specified variable or variables. In most cases, the default ascending order (from smallest to largest) is used. The variable or variables upon which to sort are specified on a BY statement that follows the PROC SORT statement.

The following are two examples of PROC SORT and BY statements:

```
PROC SORT DATA=A; BY ID;
PROC SORT DATA=FIRST; BY SOCSEC;
```

The name of the file to be sorted is placed after the DATA= part of the statement. In the first example, the file A is to be sorted; in the second example, the file FIRST is to be sorted. The variable upon which to sort is placed after the BY. In the first example, sorting will be done on the variable ID. In the second example, sorting will be done on the variable SOCSEC.

There are times when you wish to sort on two or more variables. To accomplish this, you list all sort variables on the BY statement. The order from left to right on the BY statement is the order in which the sorting will be done. For example:

```
PROC SORT DATA=FILEX; BY LOCATION RANK.
```

will sort the file FILEX by LOCATION first and then by RANK. First the cases will be listed from lowest to highest on the variable LOCATION. Then, cases with the same value for LOCATION will be sorted by RANK. Any number of variables can be placed on the BY statement.

Files can be sorted according to variables with character (non-numeric, or alphabetic) variables, such as names. There are several different sorting orders for non-numeric values, including ASCII and EBCDIC. With these orders, the case of the letters is important. The default is determined by your computer system. With ASCII order, uppercase letters are lower in the sort order than lowercase letters. With EBCDIC, the lowercase are lower than the uppercase. With names, you must be consistent in how you use upper and lower case. The names "SMITH," "Smith," and "smith" are not the same when the computer sorts them.

If you wish to sort names of people or things, a SAS program can be used to alphabetize your cases. If you have a file of names, a simple sort will accomplish this, as in

```
PROC SORT DATA=NAMEFILE; BY NAME;
```

If you follow this with a PROC PRINT, you will get a list of your cases in alphabetical order according to NAME. Just be certain that the use of upper and lower case is consistent.

Missing values are given the lowest possible rank in a sort. Thus, if some of your cases have missing values for the variable upon which you are sorting, they will come first in the sorted list. You can eliminate cases with missing values on the sort variable or variables with the appropriate statements within your program. This might require you to create a data step in which the file to be sorted is input and the appropriate cases are deleted with a DELETE statement. With the above example, you might write the following short program:

```
DATA NAMEFILE;
SET SASUSER.NAMEFILE;
IF NAME = . THEN DELETE;
PROC SORT; BY NAME;
```

It is not necessary to list the name of the file (NAMEFILE) on the PROC SORT because it immediately follows the NAMEFILE data step. The default data set for any PROC is the one most recently created before it.

INPUTTING FROM AND OUTPUTTING TO SAS DATA LIBRARY FILES

A SAS data library, as we have already discussed, can be used to save the resulting data set that is built by a data step. To review briefly, each data step will create a SAS working data set that contains all the input variables plus variables that are created or modified by your various SAS statements. The

DROP and KEEP statements can be used to control the variables that remain in the data set, and the DELETE statement can be used to eliminate cases. The SAS data set can be stored permanently in a SAS data library. The library will contain not only the data but also the variable names and the programs that created the data set. A library file can be quite convenient when there is a great deal of data manipulation to be done before statistical analysis. It is a common practice to do manipulation in one program that saves the results to a SAS data library, and then do analyses in separate programs that access the stored library. These analysis programs can often be no more than a DATA and SET statement followed by PROCs.

The procedure for creating a SAS data library varies across versions and releases of SAS. With Windows versions, you first create the SAS data library outside a SAS program, and then your program can input and output data sets from that library. For Release 8, you create a library by first clicking on the Add New Library icon on the toolbar near the top of the screen. A dialog box will appear that allows you to enter the name of the library and the location. To see your existing libraries, go to the Explorer window (see left side of Figure 1.2). For Release 6.11 click on Globals from the pulldown menu at the top of your screen (see Figure 1.1). Then click on Access and then Display libraries to get to the Libraries dialog box. From here you can see the various libraries that have been created. To make a new one, click on New Library to open the New Library dialog box. Insert the name of the library beneath Library and the folder where you wish it to be stored beneath Folder to Assign. Be sure to remember the library name because you will need to refer to it within your SAS program. With Release 6 and 8, SASUSER is a default library that is automatically created for your use. You can put all of your files in this library, or you can create other libraries.

To save (output) your data set to the library, refer to the library name and the data set name on a DATA statement, as in

```
DATA MYLIB.ELECT;
```

This statement will output the data set named ELECT to the library named MYLIB, which must already have been created before you ran this SAS program.

To input the contents of a SAS data set, use the SET statement. To read the ELECT data set from MYLIB, use the following:

```
DATA STUDY;
  SET MYLIB.ELECT;
```

This will create a working SAS data set called STUDY that will initially be identical to the permanent data set ELECT. STUDY can modify ELECT with SAS statements, or it can use it unaltered. You can also input one data set using the SET statement and save the results of the data step to another data set using the DATA statement, as in

```
DATA MYLIB.SOUTH;
  SET MYLIB.US;
```

In this case, the data set US is input, modified, and then saved as SOUTH. For example, you might create a subset of data involving only southern states from data for the entire United States.

OUTPUTTING
MULTIPLE DATA SETS

Not only can you input multiple data sets with a SAS program, but you can output multiple data sets as well. There are two approaches to accomplishing this. You can create SAS data sets, either working data sets or SAS data library data sets, or you can use FILE and PUT statements to output to non-SAS data sets.

Files to which you wish to output do not have to exist before your program is executed. The SAS System will automatically create the files if they do not exist. If the files already exist, your program will overwrite whatever is presently in them. You must be careful when using existing data sets that you in fact wish to delete the old files and re-create them. All data in the files will be lost. This is a very dangerous procedure if you wish to read data from a file and write back to the same file. If the program fails to execute properly because of a syntax or logical error, there is a good chance that everything in the original file will be lost.

Outputting to
SAS Data Sets

To output data to two or more SAS data sets, you must define them on the DATA statement from which you wish to output. To do this, you list the names of all files to which you wish to output, as in

```
DATA ONEOUT TWOOUT;
```

or

```
DATA SASUSER.ONE SASUSER.TWO;
```

Both of these statements will allow you to output cases into either or both of these files. Note that you output entire cases, as opposed to specific variables. You can use KEEP and DROP statements to select those variables to be output, but you do not have control case by case of what is output. With FILE and PUT statements, to be discussed later, you output individual variables, giving you more control over what is output.

In the first example, you are outputting to working files that will be deleted once program execution ends. In the second case, you are outputting to files that will be stored permanently in a SAS data library.

The DATA statement sets up the possible files to which you can output, and if you don't take control of outputting with the OUTPUT statement, all cases will be automatically output to all files. There are times, however, when you wish to split the cases into different files, with some going into one file and others into another. This is accomplished with OUTPUT statements in which the name of the file to be outputted to is listed, as in

```
OUTPUT ONEOUT;
```

or

```
OUTPUT TWOOUT;
```

The first statement will cause the case currently being processed to be output to the file named ONEOUT. The second statement will cause the current case to be output to the file named TWOOUT.

This feature of the SAS language allows you to place different subsets of cases into different files by use of the appropriate logical statements. Suppose you wish to put all cases with an age of 18 or greater in a file named ADULT and all cases with an age less than 18 in a file named CHILD. The following IF . . . THENs will accomplish the task:

```
IF AGE >= 18 THEN OUTPUT ADULT;
IF AGE < 18 THEN OUTPUT CHILD;
```

Outputting to Non-SAS Files

FILE and PUT statements can be used together within a data step to output to one or more non-SAS data files. Each of the files is defined on a FILE statement. Each time a FILE statement is executed, it redirects output to the file noted on it. When using multiple FILE statements, you must take care that they are placed in the appropriate places to direct output at the time you wish it directed. Each FILE statement works with one or more PUT statements. The PUT statements work as shown in prior chapters.

The following statements can be used to direct the output of one variable to one file and another variable to another file:

```
FILE 'FILEX';
PUT ID 3. X 1.;
FILE 'FILEY';
PUT ID 3. Y 2.;
```

The first file statement says to output the variables ID and X to a file named FILEX, with ID occupying three columns and X occupying one column. The second FILE statement redirects output to FILEY with ID occupying three columns and Y occupying two columns. The files written to can have partially over-lapping sets of variables as in this case, where both files had ID but the first had X and the second had Y. It is also allowable to have totally overlapping sets of variables in all files, or nonoverlapping sets with no shared variables at all.

COMBINING DATA
FROM SEVERAL FILES

A very common programming problem is to combine data from several sources for analysis. Often the data needed for a particular analysis may be spread over two or more data files. It would be very inconvenient, and a waste of time, to print the contents of each file and then reenter the needed data into a file for analysis. It is far easier to write a SAS program to pull together the data from each file.

For illustrative purposes, suppose that you are interested in studying the relation between student GPA and later work success as reflected in salary level. Further suppose that you have access to survey data on two cohorts of graduates from the same university. Each cohort's data, which include salary, are contained in a separate data file. Data on grade point average (GPA) can be found in the university's computer database of alumni. Presume that all data files contain each graduate's social security number.

To accomplish this programming task, you must first concatenate the two cohort files into a single file of salary data. Next you must merge the file con-taining salary data with the file containing GPA. Finally, you might wish to save the resulting file in a SAS data library for future analysis.

Program 8.1 shows the SAS statements to accomplish this task, and Table 8.2 shows the two files that contain the salary data for the first and second cohort, and the file that contains GPA. Lines 1 to 4 of the program create the SAS data set ONE and input the social security number (SSN) and salary from COHORT1.DAT. Likewise, lines 5 to 8 create the SAS data set TWO and input the social security number and salary from COHORT2.DAT. Note that the variable COHORT was created in lines 4 and 8 to keep track of the cohort number for each case. Lines 9 and 10 concatenate the SAS data sets ONE and TWO into the SAS data set BOTH. Line 11 PROC PRINTs the contents of BOTH, which can be seen in Output 8.1.

Program 8.1

```
1    DATA ONE;
2       INFILE 'A:COHORT1.DAT';
3       INPUT SSN 9. SALARY 5.;
4       COHORT = 1;
5    DATA TWO;
6       INFILE 'A:COHORT2.DAT';
7       INPUT SSN 9. SALARY 5.;
8       COHORT = 2;
9    DATA BOTH;
10      SET ONE TWO;
11      PROC PRINT;
12   DATA GRADES;
13      INFILE 'A:GPA.DAT';
14      INPUT SSN 9. GPA 2.1;
15      PROC SORT DATA = BOTH;BY SSN;
16      PROC SORT DATA = GRADES;BY SSN;
17   DATA COMBINE;
18      MERGE BOTH GRADES;BY SSN;
19      PROC PRINT;
20   DATA SASUSER.SALGPA;
21      SET COMBINE;
22   RUN;
```

The next part of the program merges BOTH, which now contains all the available cases, with the file containing the GPA data. Lines 12 to 14 input the social security number (SSN) and GPA into the SAS data set GRADES. Lines 15 and 16 sort the two data sets by social security number so that they can be merged. The merging is accomplished in lines 17 and 18. The contents of the resulting data set COMBINE is output with a PROC PRINT (line 19). The output from the PROC PRINT is also shown in Output 8.1. Finally, the contents of COMBINE are saved to a SAS data library in a data set called SASUSER.SALGPA. Note that for the PC version SASUSER is the name of a subdirectory that has been set up to hold all SAS data library files. How the library file is set up depends on your particular computer system.

The creation of data sets from step to step can be traced in the SAS Log (see Log 8.1). The log shows the blocks of statements from each data step and

Table 8.2

Contents of COHORT1.DAT

```
12235172032000
03552189418000
83948193145000
15251558021000
73007807148000
```

Contents of COHORT2.DAT

```
31961902221000
77693918517000
25188403958000
20821208016000
19333371940000
```

Contents of GPA.DAT

```
12235172037
03552189427
83948193135
15251558034
73007807136
31961902225
77693918522
25188403939
20821208021
19333371929
```

gives a message indicating the number of cases and variables for each data set. It is essential that you carefully inspect the SAS Log when you manipulate multiple files to be certain that the proper number of cases and variables have been input and output from the various data sets. The log will also indicate when data set creation has failed by noting that a data set has no cases or no variables.

Output 8.1

The SAS System

OBS	SSN	SALARY	COHORT1
1	122351720	32000	1
2	35521894	18000	1
3	839481931	45000	1
4	152515580	21000	1
5	730078071	48000	1
6	319619022	21000	2
7	776939185	17000	2
8	251884039	58000	2
9	208212080	16000	2
10	193333719	40000	2

OBS	SSN	SALARY	COHORT	GPA
1	35521894	18000	1	2.7
2	122351720	32000	1	3.7
3	152515580	21000	1	3.4
4	193333719	40000	2	2.9
5	208212080	16000	2	2.1
6	251884039	58000	2	3.9
7	319619022	21000	2	2.5
8	730078071	48000	1	3.6
9	776939185	17000	2	2.2
10	839481931	45000	1	3.5

CREATING MULTIPLE FILES

Another fairly common task is to take a large file and divide it into two or more smaller files. This might occur because it would be easier to handle smaller files, or because you are sharing a subset of data with another researcher. Subfiles can include all variables on subsets of cases, subsets of variables on all cases, or subsets of variables on subsets of cases.

For the current example, the SAS data library file created in Program 8.1 is divided back into the two individual cohort files. These two files will contain all the variables pulled together by Program 8.1, that is, social security number,

Log 8.1

```
The SAS System

    DATA ONE;
      INFILE 'A:COHORT1.DAT';
      INPUT SSN 9. SALARY 5.;
      COHORT = 1;
    DATA TWO;
NOTE: The infile 'A:COHORT1.DAT' is file A:\COHORT1.DAT.
NOTE: 5 records were read from the infile A:\COHORT1.DAT.
  The minimum record length was 14.
  The maximum record length was 14.
NOTE: The data set WORK.ONE has 5 observations and 3 variables.
NOTE: The DATA statement used 4.00 seconds.
      INFILE 'A:COHORT2.DAT';
      INPUT SSN 9. SALARY 5.;
      COHORT = 2;
    DATA BOTH;
NOTE: The infile 'A:COHORT2.DAT' is file A:\COHORT2.DAT.
NOTE: 5 records were read from the infile A:\COHORT2.DAT.
  The minimum record length was 14.
  The maximum record length was 14.
NOTE: The data set WORK.TWO has 5 observations and 3 variables.
NOTE: The DATA statement used 5.00 seconds.
      SET ONE TWO;
    PROC PRINT;
NOTE: The data set WORK.BOTH has 10 observations and 3 variables.
NOTE: The DATA statement used 2.00 seconds.
      DATA GRADES;
NOTE: The PROCEDURE PRINT used 1.00 seconds.
        INFILE 'A:GPA.DAT';
        INPUT SSN 9. GPA 2.1;
      PROC SORT DATA = BOTH;BY SSN;
NOTE: The infile 'A:GPA.DAT' is file A:\GPA.DAT.
NOTE: 10 records were read from the infile A:\GPA.DAT.
  The minimum record length was 11.
  The maximum record length was 11.
NOTE: The data set WORK.GRADES has 10 observations and 2 variables.
NOTE: The DATA statement used 5.00 seconds.
      PROC SORT DATA = GRADES;BY SSN;
NOTE: The data set WORK.BOTH has 10 observations and 3 variables.
NOTE: The PROCEDURE SORT used 1.00 seconds.
      DATA COMBINE;
NOTE: The data set WORK.GRADES has 10 observations and 2 variables.
NOTE: The PROCEDURE SORT used 1.00 seconds.
        MERGE BOTH GRADES;BY SSN;
      PROC PRINT;
```

(continued)

```
(Continued)

NOTE: The data set WORK.COMBINE has 10 observations and 4
  variables.
NOTE: The DATA statement used 2.00 seconds.
    DATA SASUSER.SALGPA;
NOTE: The PROCEDURE PRINT used 2.00 seconds.
      SET COMBINE;
    RUN;
NOTE: The data set SASUSER.SALGPA has 10 observations and 4
  variables.
NOTE: The DATA statement used 3.00 seconds.
```

salary, GPA, and cohort number. The program illustrates two ways of splitting the files. First, it shows how to create two SAS data sets, one for each cohort. Next, it shows how to create two non-SAS data files, one for each cohort. In the first case, the data are output with a PROC PRINT. In the second case, the output is directed to PRINT, but it could have been directed to files.

The first data step in Program 8.2 creates two SAS data sets, COH1 and COH2 (line 1). Next, data are input from the SAS data set SASUSER.SALGPA, which is contained in the SAS data library (line 2).

The next two statements (lines 3 and 4) output the cases into their appropriate SAS data sets, depending upon their value for the variable COHORT.

Program 8.2

```
1   DATA COH1 COH2;
2   SET SASUSER.SALGPA;
3   IF COHORT = 1 THEN OUTPUT COH1;
4   IF COHORT = 2 THEN OUTPUT COH2;
5   PROC PRINT DATA = COH1;
6   PROC PRINT DATA = COH2;
7   DATA SPLIT;
8   SET SASUSER.SALGPA;
9   FILE PRINT;
10  IF COHORT = 1 THEN PUT @5 SSN;
11  IF COHORT = 2 THEN PUT @15 SSN;
12  RUN;
```

Output 8.2

```
The SAS System

        OBS  SSN       SALARY  COHORT  GPA
         1   35521894   18000    1     2.7
         2  122351720   32000    1     3.7
         3  152515580   21000    1     3.4
         4  730078071   48000    1     3.6
         5  839481931   45000    1     3.5

        OBS  SSN       SALARY  COHORT  GPA
         1  193333719   40000    2     2.9
         2  208212080   16000    2     2.1
         3  251884039   58000    2     3.9
         4  319619022   21000    2     2.5
         5  776939185   17000    2     2.2

35521894
122351720
152515580
                193333719
                208212080
                251884039
                319619022
730078071
                776939185
839481931
```

The results are output with the PROC PRINTs in lines 5 and 6 and can be seen in Output 8.2.

The second data step creates a SAS data set SPLIT (line 7) and inputs SASUSER.SALGPA. Lines 10 and 11 output the cases. For illustrative purposes, the cases are output into two columns beginning at column 5 and 15 of the page. Cohort 1 is in the left-hand column, and Cohort 2 is in the right-hand column. Normally you would direct output to two files with file statements that would precede the PUT statements. Both the FILE and PUT statements could be placed after a DO statement, as in

Program 8.3

```
1    DATA MISS;
2       INPUT ID 1. (X1-X8) (1.);
3       ARRAY X(8) X1-X8;
4       DO I = 1 TO 8;
5         IF X(I) = . THEN DELETE;
6       END;
7       FILE PRINT;
8       PUT @5 ID 1. @ 10 (X1-X8) (1.);
9    DATALINES;
112345678
21234 678
31 345678
42234 687
587654321
;
     RUN;
```

```
IF COHORT = 1 THEN DO;
  FILE 'COHORT1.DAT';
  PUT SSN SALARY GPA;
END;
```

Deleting Cases With Missing Values

Program 8.3 reads a file, deletes cases with missing data, and outputs the remaining file. Line 2 inputs the variables ID and X1 to X8. Line 3 places the X variables into an array for easier processing. The loop in lines 4 to 6 checks each of the eight X variables to see if there is a missing value. If so, the case is dropped with the DELETE statement. The FILE PRINT (line 7) and PUT (line 8) statements output the ID and eight X variables for only those cases not deleted in the loop.

Output 8.3

```
The SAS System
   1     12345678
   5     87654321
```

The input data are placed after the DATALINES statement. As you can see, only the first and last case had complete data on all variables. Output 8.3 shows that only these two cases were output.

This program could be modified to accomplish other manipulations of files, including sorting or duplicating a file from one location to another. To sort a file, you would input it with one data step, sort it with a PROC SORT, input the sorted file into another data step, and output the results. Program 8.4 is a skeleton of such a program, which you could expand for an actual application.

To move a file, you would input it from one file and output it to another. The skeleton of a program to accomplish this is shown as Program 8.5. Note that each character is read one at a time and that character rather than numeric format is used. This is necessary to ensure that the output file will match the input file. The single character avoids problems caused by leading zeros and blanks within a data set. For example, if you read a two-digit number, if you input a "02," the SAS program may output it as " 2," dropping the leading zero. Thus, the output file will not exactly match the input. The use of character values avoids a problem caused by how missing values are processed with numeric variables. Any missing numeric value is converted to a period

Program 8.4
Program to Create a Sorted Version of a File

```
DATA SORTFILE;
   INFILE . . . ;
   INPUT  . . . ;
PROC SORT; BY . . . ;
DATA SORTED;
   SET SORTFILE;
   FILE . . . ;
   PUT . . . ;
```

Program 8.5
Program to Duplicate a File

```
DATA DUP;
   INFILE . . . ;
   INPUT (X1-X50) ($1.);
   FILE . . . ;
   PUT (X1-X50) ($1.);
```

(".”). If there are missing values in the data set, as is usually the case, the output file will be sprinkled with periods. With character format, a blank remains a blank.

COMMON ERRORS

When combining and dividing files, the SAS Log messages are critical because they indicate how many cases and variables were in the original inputted files and how many are in the outputted files. These provide vital information about whether or not the files have been properly combined or divided. Of course, you must go beyond this in checking to be sure the correct variables were input and output, and here the PROC PRINT can be helpful when run on each file. If the files are large, the number of cases printed can be limited.

Another trouble spot has to do with merging. Be sure that you included the BY statement to match cases appropriately. If you forget the BY, cases will be matched up in order. This is fine if each file has the same cases in the same order, but if even one is missing, the cases will become scrambled. It is always safest to include the BY rather than hope everything will match.

∽ Debugging Exercises ∽

Exercise 8.1

```
    *Program to concatenate two files. Note
the second file has a variable not con-
tained in the first;
    data file1;
    input id party;
    datalines;
    0011 demo
    0065 indep
    8796 green
    7659 demo
    6567 repub
    4345 indep
    ;
    data file2;
    input id party voted;
    datalines;
    0876 demo yes
    8866 demo no
    5453 repub no
    3442 repub yes
    ;
    data combine;
    merge file1 file2;
    proc print;
    run;
```

Exercise 8.2

```
   *Program to merge two files that contain
different variables.;
   data file1;
   input id party $;
   datalines;
0011 demo
0065 indep
8796 green
7659 demo
6567 repub
4345 indep
;
   data file2;
   input id voted $;
   datalines;
7659 yes
6567 yes
4345 yes
0011 yes
0065 no
8796 no
;
   data combine;
   merge file1 file2;
   proc print;
   run;
```

Chapter 9

Using SAS® PROCs

One of the strengths of the SAS system is the library of built-in statistical procedures or PROCs. PROCs can perform most of the statistical tests and procedures researchers are likely to need. They can also output results to a file so that they can be input into a data step for further analysis. For example, it is possible to input raw data, compute the correlations among a number of variables, and output the correlation values to a file for further analysis. This chapter will cover a sample of PROCs that compute both simple and complex statistics. On the simple side are PROCs to compute descriptive statistics, two-way contingency tables, correlations, and *t* tests. The chapter will also discuss how to produce simple graphs such as scatterplots. Complex statistics will include multiple regression, analysis of variance (ANOVA), factorial analysis of variance (ANOVA), and factor analysis. It is not my intent to provide a detailed statistics primer, but rather to provide examples to illustrate how PROCs can be used.

Every PROC must be run in conjunction with a SAS data set. The data set can be created within the current program, or it can exist in a permanent SAS data library. If data exist in a non-SAS data file, a program must be written to input the variables into a SAS data set before a PROC can be run.

PROCs, as opposed to SAS functions, cannot be run inside a data step. Once a PROC statement is encountered, SAS terminates the data step. Subsequent data steps can follow a PROC, and it is not uncommon to begin a program with a data step to prepare data for analysis, conduct the analysis with a PROC that outputs some of its results, and then to manipulate the output from the PROC with another data step. It is a common error to embed a PROC inside a data step.

PROCs allow you to specify the SAS data set to be analyzed. If the data set is left unspecified, the most recently mentioned data set is the one assumed. PROCs also allow you to list the variables to be analyzed. In some PROCs, it is necessary to specify variables for analysis. In others, like PROC CORR or PROC MEANS, every variable in the data set will be analyzed, unless otherwise specified.

In the following examples, the use of five basic PROCs and two advanced PROCs will be illustrated. Specifically covered will be PROC CORR, PROC FREQ, PROC MEANS, PROC PLOT, and PROC TTEST to conduct simple analyses. PROC ANOVA, PROC REG, PROC GLM, and PROC FACTOR will be used to conduct more complex analyses. Each will be applied to the same data set, which is from an actual survey of university clerical workers.

TURNOVER AMONG UNIVERSITY CLERICAL WORKERS[1]

The reactions people have to their jobs has been a topic of much interest in several disciplines within the social sciences. A particular focus for study has been how people feel about their jobs and how those feelings are related to quitting the job, or turnover. The examples in this chapter make use of data from a survey concerning people's feelings about their jobs and about quitting their jobs, and information about whether or not they actually quit.

The respondents to this survey were 156 clerical employees of the University of South Florida. All respondents were women who worked in either academic departments, administration, or support services. Several types of clerical positions were represented in the sample, including secretaries, administrative assistants, and clerks. The survey was conducted in the summer of 1986. About 15 months later, a follow-up was conducted to determine which of the respondents had quit their jobs.

Data from the survey assessed job satisfaction, job frustration, intention to quit the job, age, and length of tenure on the job. Job satisfaction was measured with a three-item scale from the Michigan Organizational Assessment

Scale (Cammann, Fichman, Jenkins, & Klesh, 1979). This scale measures how much the respondent likes his or her job. Frustration was measured with the three-item Peters and O'Connor (1980) scale. It assesses the extent to which a person feels frustrated at work. Intent to quit was measured with a single six-choice item that asked how often the person intended to quit his or her job. Age was indicated in years, and tenure was indicated in months. Turnover data were gathered from a directory of university employees by checking a year after the survey was completed to see who was no longer there.

To make subsequent analysis easier, a program was written to input the data, score the two scales, and save the data in a permanent SAS data library. The program is shown as Program 9.1. It uses the programming features discussed in the earlier chapters, so there should be nothing here that is new. It looks much like Program 7.1, which scored a psychological test.

The program inputs the data from a file named TURNOVER.DAT (see line 3). It inputs the six items from the frustration and satisfaction scales, the one intent item, the turnover status, age, and tenure. Lines 10 to 12 reverse score the first and third items for the frustration scale, as well as the first item for the satisfaction scale. The loop at lines 14 to 16 converts the missing items to zeros so that the nonmissing items can be summed later. The loops at lines 18 to 21 and 23 to 26 score the frustration and satisfaction scales, respectively. Lines 28 and 29 adjust the scores with missing items to full length. Because the data set was given a two-part name SASUSER.SURVEY in line 1, the data set will be saved to a permanent SAS data library. In subsequent examples, data will be input from the SAS data library with a SET statement.

CORRELATIONS WITH PROC CORR

PROC CORR can be used to compute correlations between two or more variables. It also outputs descriptive statistics for each variable, including the mean, standard deviation, minimum value, and maximum value. It can output both corrected and uncorrected sum of squares and cross products. PROC CORR can be used to compute coefficient alpha for a set of test items. It can also compute partial correlations. Finally, there are options to compute different types of correlations, including Pearson, Spearman, and Kendall.

Program 9.2 computes the correlations among four variables: frustration, satisfaction, intention of quitting, and age. This example does not make use of

Program 9.1
Program to Create a SAS Library File of Survey Data

```
1   DATA SASUSER.SURVEY;
2   *Program to score turnover survey data.;
3   INFILE 'C:TURNOVER.DAT';
4   INPUT ID 3. (ITEM1-ITEM6) (1.) INTENT 1. QUIT 1. AGE 2. TENURE 3.;
5   KEEP ID ITEM1-ITEM6 INTENT QUIT AGE TENURE FRUST SATIS;
6   ARRAY ITEM(6) ITEM1-ITEM6;
7   *Initialize counters and accumulators.;
8   FTOT = 0; FRUST = 0; STOT = 0; SATIS = 0;
9   *Reverse item scoring.;
10  ITEM1 = 7-ITEM1;
11  ITEM3 = 7-ITEM3;
12  ITEM4 = 7-ITEM4;
13  *Convert missing values to zeros.;
14  DO I = 1 TO 6;
15    IF ITEM(I) = . THEN ITEM(I) = 0;
16  END;
17  *Score frustration scale.;
18  DO I = 1 TO 3;
19    IF ITEM(I) > 0 THEN FTOT = FTOT + 1;
20    FRUST = FRUST + ITEM(I);
21  END;
22  *Score satisfaction scale.;
23  DO I = 4 TO 6;
24    IF ITEM(I) > 0 THEN STOT = STOT + 1;
25    SATIS = SATIS + ITEM(I);
26  END;
27  *Adjust for number of items.;
28  FRUST = FRUST / FTOT * 3;
29  SATIS = SATIS / STOT * 3;
30  RUN;
```

the data step. The PROC CORR statement itself specifies the name of the SAS data set to be input.

The program contains only two lines. The first indicates that PROC CORR is to be run on the SAS data set named SURVEY that is contained in the permanent SAS data library named SASUSER. The second line indicates the variables to be analyzed. Output 9.2 contains the output from the PROC. Near the top of the output, the section labeled "Simple Statistics" contains each variable's descriptive statistics of sample size, mean, standard deviation, sum of scores across subjects, and the minimum and maximum values. Below the descriptive

---

Program 9.2

Program to Compute Correlations

```
1 PROC CORR DATA=SASUSER.SURVEY;
2    VAR FRUST SATIS INTENT AGE;
3 RUN;
```

---

statistics are the correlations organized into a matrix. For each variable pair, the matrix shows the value of the correlation, the exact probability level for the correlation, and the sample size. Because of missing data, sample sizes are not the same for each correlation.

Note that unless otherwise specified, the default for PROC CORR is **pairwise deletion**. This means that for each correlation, every case that has values for both variables will be included. With missing values spread throughout a data set, this will result in different sample sizes for different correlations. An optional setting is **listwise deletion**, where a case is deleted from all correlation calculations if missing values exist for any variable. In many data sets, there are few or no cases with complete data. In cases where pairwise deletion may allow for sufficient sample size, listwise deletion may not. For some complex analyses, like multiple regression or multivariate analysis of variance, listwise deletion is necessary.

FREQUENCY TABLES
WITH PROC FREQ

PROC FREQ provides counts of the number of cases that have each possible value of a variable, or combinations of values of two or more variables. The number or frequency of cases is placed in a table. For two-way tables of frequencies of all possible combinations of two variables, significance tests and measures of association are provided.

For the turnover example, two types of frequency tables were computed. First, one-way tables were used to show the distribution of age in the sample. The table indicated how many cases were at each of the observed ages in the

Output 9.2

The SAS System

CORRELATION ANALYSIS

4 'VAR' Variables: FRUST   SATIS   INTENT   AGE

Simple Statistics

Variable	N	Mean	Std Dev	Sum
FRUST	156	10.42308	4.2199	1626
SATIS	156	14.6987	3.2377	2293.0
INTENT	155	2.8710	1.3470	445.0
AGE	153	40.6209	10.8276	6215.0

CORRELATION ANALYSIS

Simple Statistics

Variable	Minimum	Maximum
FRUST	3.0000	18.0000
SATIS	3.0000	18.0000
INTENT	1.0000	6.0000
AGE	23.0000	70.0000

CORRELATION ANALYSIS

Pearson Correlation Coefficients / Prob > |R|
under Ho: Rho=0
/ Number of Observations

	FRUST	SATIS	INTENT	AGE
FRUST	1.00000	-0.52506	0.57146	-0.04268
	0.0	0.0001	0.0001	0.6011
	156	156	155	153
SATIS	-0.52506	1.00000	-0.69714	0.05918
	0.0001	0.0	0.0001	0.4674
	156	156	155	153

(continued)

(continued)

INTENT	0.57146	-0.69714	1.00000	-0.27384
	0.0001	0.0001	0.0	0.0006
	155	155	155	152

CORRELATION ANALYSIS

Pearson Correlation Coefficients / Prob > |R| under Ho:
Rho=0
/ Number of Observations

	FRUST	SATIS	INTENT	AGE
AGE	-0.04268	0.05918	-0.27384	1.00000
	0.6011	0.4674	0.0006	0.0
	153	153	152	153

sample. The second type of table was a two-way contingency table showing the relation of turnover itself to intention to quit. Because turnover had two levels (quit or didn't quit) and intention of quitting had six levels (ranging from *never* to *extremely often*), the table was a two × six. As an option, tests for significant association between turnover and quitting were output.

Program 9.3 produces both types of frequency tables. Note that this time the data were input into a working SAS data set with a data step. Line 3 used a Round function to create age categories. Because of the way in which Round works, this function will create 10-year categories, for example from 15 to 24, 25 to 34, 35 to 44, and so on. The TABLES statement in line 5 specifies two one-way tables, one for the variable AGE and the other for AGECAT.

The first PROC FREQ statement creates the two one-way frequency tables in Output 9.3a. The table lists the values for AGE in the first column. As can be seen, age ranges in this sample from 23 to 70. The second column lists the number of cases that have each value of age. The third column is the percentage of cases in the sample that have each value of age. The fourth column is the cumulative frequency from the lowest to highest value. Each entry indicates the number of cases that has the current or lower value. The last column is the cumulative percentage, or the percentage of cases that has the current or lower value. A note at the bottom of the table indicates the number of missing cases.

Program 9.3
Program to Compute Frequency Tables

```
1   DATA FREQTBL;
2     SET SASUSER.SURVEY;
3     AGECAT = ROUND(AGE,10);
4   PROC FREQ;
5     TABLES AGE AGECAT;
6   RUN;
7   DATA FREQTBL;
8     SET SASUSER.SURVEY;
9   PROC FREQ;
10    TABLES QUIT * INTENT/CHISQ;
11  RUN;
```

The second table in Output 9.3a is for the variable AGECAT. The table's structure is similar to that of the previous table. In this case, there are only six possible values, which represent age categories. The use of the age categories makes interpretation easier than using the original age variable. This is because there are many possible values for age and a small number of cases for most individual ages. Other age categories could be created within the data step.

The two-way table shown in Output 9.3b was generated by the second PROC FREQ statement in Program 9.3. To produce a two-way table, the two variables of interest are listed in the TABLES statement (line 10) with an asterisk between them. The CHISQ specification causes a chi-square significance test to be output.

In the two-way table, the columns represent values of INTENT, which can range from 1 (never) to 6 (extremely often). The rows represent the two levels of turnover, 0 (Didn't quit) and 1 (Quit). The table was broken into four parts, which unfortunately makes the results not very readable. It is unlikely that this table format could be used in a report or article. This table structure, however, contains all cell and marginal means, as well as percentages that each cell is of the total cases, of all cases in the particular row, and of all cases in the particular column.

The first part of the table contains data for the nonquitters who had values of 1, 2, or 3 for intention of quitting. The uppermost number in each cell is the

Output 9.3a

The SAS System

AGE	Frequency	Percent	Cumulative Frequency	Cumulative Percent
23	1	0.7	1	0.7
24	4	2.6	5	3.3
25	3	2.0	8	5.2
26	4	2.6	12	7.8
27	7	4.6	19	12.4
28	6	3.9	25	16.3
29	6	3.9	31	20.3
30	2	1.3	33	21.6
31	4	2.6	37	24.2
32	2	1.3	39	25.5
33	3	2.0	42	27.5
34	4	2.6	46	30.1
35	8	5.2	54	35.3
36	9	5.9	63	41.2
37	2	1.3	65	42.5
38	7	4.6	72	47.1
39	7	4.6	79	51.6
40	4	2.6	83	54.2
41	5	3.3	88	57.5
42	2	1.3	90	58.8
43	5	3.3	95	62.1
44	8	5.2	103	67.3
45	2	1.3	105	68.6
46	5	3.3	110	71.9
47	1	0.7	111	72.5
48	4	2.6	115	75.2
49	3	2.0	118	77.1
50	5	3.3	123	80.4
51	3	2.0	126	82.4
52	3	2.0	129	84.3
53	3	2.0	132	86.3
54	1	0.7	133	86.9
55	3	2.0	136	88.9
56	1	0.7	137	89.5
57	4	2.6	141	92.2

(continued)

(Continued)

58	4	2.6	145	94.8
59	1	0.7	146	95.4
61	1	0.7	147	96.1
62	1	0.7	148	96.7
63	2	1.3	150	98.0
66	1	0.7	151	98.7
67	1	0.7	152	99.3
70	1	0.7	153	100.0

Frequency Missing = 3

AGECAT	Frequency	Percent	Cumulative Frequency	Cumulative Percent
20	5	3.3	5	3.3
30	41	26.8	46	30.1
40	57	37.3	103	67.3
50	30	19.6	133	86.9
60	17	11.1	150	98.0
70	3	2.0	153	100.0

Frequency Missing = 3

number of cases that had that combination of values. For example, the left-most cell, which represented nonquitters who never considered quitting, had 20 respondents. To the right of the table, under the heading " Total," is the total number of cases (117) with a value of 0 for QUIT. This represented 75.48% of the total cases. Below each of the cells are the totals for each value of INTENT. Thus, there were 24 cases with a value of 1 for INTENT, 40 cases with a value of 2, and 53 cases with a value of 3. Below the frequencies are the percentages of total cases with each value of INTENT. Thus, 15.48% of total cases had a value of 1, 25.81% had a value of 2, and 34.19% had a value of 3. The rightmost and lowermost value in the table (155) is the total number of cases.

Within each cell, below the frequency, are three percentages. The first is the percentage that the cell frequency is of the total number of cases. For the leftmost cell, 20 respondents represent 12.9% of the 155 total respondents. The next percentage is the percentage that the cell frequency is of the total number of cases with a value of 0 for QUIT. Thus, 20 is 17.09% of the 117 cases

Output 9.3b

The SAS System

TABLE OF QUIT BY INTENT

QUIT   INTENT

```
Frequency|
Percent  |
Row Pct  |
Col Pct  |       1|       2|       3|   Total
```

	1	2	3	Total
0	20	35	36	117
	12.90	22.58	23.23	75.48
	17.09	29.91	30.77	
	83.33	87.50	67.92	

Total	24	40	53	155
	15.48	25.81	34.19	100.00

(Continued)

TABLE OF QUIT BY INTENT

QUIT   INTENT

```
Frequency|
Percent  |
Row Pct  |
Col Pct  |       1|       2|       3|   Total
```

	1	2	3	Total
1	4	5	17	38
	2.58	3.23	10.97	24.52
	10.53	13.16	44.74	
	16.67	12.50	32.08	

Total	24	40	53	155
	15.48	25.81	34.19	100.00

(continued)

(continued)

```
                        TABLE OF QUIT BY INTENT

        QUIT          INTENT

        Frequency|
        Percent  |
        Row Pct  |
        Col Pct  |        4|        5|        6|      Total

               0 |      14 |       8 |       4 |        117
                 |    9.03 |    5.16 |    2.58 |      75.48
                 |   11.97 |    6.84 |    3.42 |
                 |   82.35 |   66.67 |   44.44 |

        Total            17         12          9         155
                      10.97       7.74       5.81      100.00
```

(Continued)

```
                        TABLE OF QUIT BY INTENT

        QUIT          INTENT

        Frequency|
        Percent  |
        Row Pct  |
        Col Pct  |        4|        5|        6|      Total

               1 |       3 |       4 |       5 |         38
                 |    1.94 |    2.58 |    3.23 |      24.52
                 |    7.89 |   10.53 |   13.16 |
                 |   17.65 |   33.33 |   55.56 |

        Total            17         12          9         155
                      10.97       7.74       5.81      100.00

        Frequency Missing = 1
```

(continued)

(continued)

STATISTICS FOR TABLE OF QUIT BY INTENT

Statistic	DF	Value	Prob
Chi-Square	5	11.180	0.048
Likelihood Ratio Chi-Square	5	10.894	0.054
Mantel-Haenszel Chi-Square	1	6.159	0.013
Phi Coefficient		0.269	
Contingency Coefficient		0.259	
Cramer's V		0.269	

Effective Sample Size = 155
Frequency Missing = 1
WARNING: 25% of the cells have expected counts less
          than 5. ChiSquare may not be a valid test.

that did not quit. The last number represents the percentage that the cell frequency is of the total number of cases with a value of 1 for INTENT. The 20 cases are 83.33% of the 24 respondents who indicated they never intended to quit.

The next part of the table contains those respondents who quit and had values of 1 to 3 for INTENT. Note that the column totals are the same as for the first part of the table. This is because the same three values of INTENT are represented. The row total this time represent the number of respondents (38) who quit the job. The next two sections of the table contain the frequencies for the values 4 to 6 of INTENT.

The final part of the output contains the significance tests and tests of association. It was produced because of the CHISQ option placed in line 10. It indicates the chi-square value and exact probability, as well as two other significance tests. Three measures of association—Phi, Contingency coefficient, and Cramer's V—are provided. At the bottom of the table, a warning message indicates that there are too many cells of the table with small expected frequencies. The chi-square is likely to be inaccurate in this case. To get a better inferential test, you could combine some of the categories for INTENT, perhaps collapsing the six categories to three.

DESCRIPTIVE STATISTICS
WITH PROC MEANS

The next step of the analysis of these data was to compute descriptive statistics for the individual items of the frustration and job satisfaction scales. PROC MEANS was used to compute these statistics, which could also be computed with PROC CORR. In this case, however, intercorrelations were not of interest.

Program 9.4 inputs the SAS data set SURVEY from the SAS data library SASUSER. Line 3 indicates that PROC MEANS should compute the descriptive statistics of sample size, mean, variance, standard deviation, range, and minimum and maximum values for each specified variable. Line 4 indicates that the variables of ITEM1 to ITEM6 should be analyzed.

Output 9.4 contains the descriptive statistics generated by PROC MEANS. For each variable, the descriptive statistics listed above were placed into a table. Additional descriptive statistics are also available, although there may be differences in which ones are available in different versions of the SAS System.

SCATTERPLOTS WITH PROC PLOT

The correlation between intent to quit and job satisfaction was computed by PROC CORR (Program 9.2). It is often of interest, however, to inspect the scatterplot of individual observations when a correlation is computed. PROC PLOT creates a number of different types of plots involving two variables, including scatterplots.

Program 9.4
Program to Compute Means

```
1 DATA MEANS;
2   SET SASUSER.SURVEY;
3 PROC MEANS N MEAN VAR STD RANGE MIN MAX;
4   VAR ITEM1-ITEM6;
5 RUN;
```

Output 9.4

```
The SAS System

N Obs    Variable   N    Minimum      Maximum        Range

  156    ITEM1    156    2.0000000    7.0000000    5.0000000
         ITEM2    155    1.0000000    6.0000000    5.0000000
         ITEM3    156    2.0000000    7.0000000    5.0000000
         ITEM4    155    1.0000000    6.0000000    5.0000000
         ITEM5    155    1.0000000    6.0000000    5.0000000
         ITEM6    156    1.0000000    6.0000000    5.0000000


N Obs    Variable       Mean        Variance      Std Dev

  156    ITEM1       4.5064103     2.5096361    1.5841831
         ITEM2       3.4258065     2.6227063    1.6194772
         ITEM3       4.4871795     2.6901572    1.6401699
         ITEM4       5.0645161     1.3594470    1.1659533
         ITEM5       4.6258065     1.7162128    1.3100431
         ITEM6       4.9935897     1.1160877    1.0564505
```

Program 9.5 shows how PROC PLOT can be used to create a scatterplot. Line 4 of the program specifies a plot of intention to quit (INTENT) by job satisfaction (SATIS). Output 9.5 shows the result. The letters represent the number of cases with each combination of values. A represents 1 case, B represents 2 cases, C represents 3, and so on.

Program 9.5
Program to Plot Intent by Satisfaction

```
1 DATA TURNOVER;
2    SET SASUSER.SURVEY;
3 PROC PLOT;
4    PLOT INTENT*SATIS;
5 RUN;
```

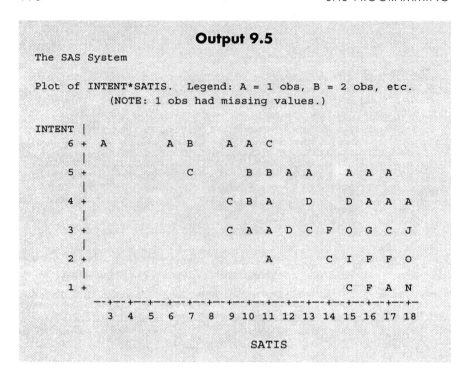

Output 9.5

```
The SAS System

Plot of INTENT*SATIS.   Legend: A = 1 obs, B = 2 obs, etc.
               (NOTE: 1 obs had missing values.)

INTENT |
    6 +  A           A  B      A  A  C
       |
    5 +               C         B  B  A  A      A  A  A
       |
    4 +                          C  B  A     D      D  A  A
       |
    3 +                          C  A  A  D  C  F  O  G  C  J
       |
    2 +                             A           C  I  F  F  O
       |
    1 +                                            C  F  A  N
       --+--+--+--+--+--+--+--+--+--+--+--+--+--+--+--+--+--+--
         3  4  5  6  7  8  9 10 11 12 13 14 15 16 17 18

                              SATIS
```

PROC PLOT allows you to customize the plot somewhat to change its appearance. It also allows you to graph one variable as a function of another. Contour plots involving three variables are also available.

t TESTS WITH PROC TTEST

The final simple analyses conducted on the turnover data were a series of *t* tests comparing the quitters and nonquitters on four variables: frustration, job satisfaction, intention to quit, and age. PROC TTEST computes both descriptive statistics and *t* tests to compare groups.

Program 9.6 shows the statements necessary to run PROC TTEST. Line 4 indicates the independent variable, in this example QUIT. Line 5 specifies the dependent variables,
FRUST, SATIS, INTENT, and AGE.

Program 9.6
Program to Compute *t* Tests

```
1 DATA TTEST;
2   SET SASUSER.SURVEY;
3 PROC TTEST;
4   CLASS QUIT;
5   VAR FRUST SATIS INTENT AGE;
6 RUN;
```

Output 9.6 shows the results of the program from Release 8 (output for Release 6 is organized differently and doesn't show the confidence intervals). The first table contains descriptive statistics. It is a bit busy, as it contains the means, standard deviations, and standard errors for each group (called class) and their difference. Not only are the overall group statistics given, but 95% confidence intervals are shown as well. These can be eliminated with the option on the PROC TTEST command of "ci = none." The second table contains two types of *t* tests. Pooled are for cases with equal variances between both groups. Satterthwaite are adjusted for unequal sample sizes. In this example, results are almost identical with the two types. The final table contains tests for the homogeneity of variance between the two groups. Although not shown here, PROC TTEST can be used for dependent (matched group) *t* tests as well.

As can be seen, the *t* test for frustration, the first variable output, is nonsignificant. The variances were not significantly heterogeneous, resulting in the two *t* tests being quite close in value. The remaining three *t* tests were significant, with nonquitters being more satisfied (mean = 15.0 vs. 13.7), having less intention to quit (mean = 2.7 vs. 3.3), and being older (mean = 41.9 vs. 36.8) than quitters. Note that the means were all rounded here.

COMPLEX STATISTICS

Running more complex statistics can be no more difficult than simple statistics. Program 9.7 conducts four different analyses. The program reads data from the file SURVEY that was located in the SAS data library SASUSER. The tenure variable was converted from months to years, then rounded, in the 3rd state-

Output 9.6

The SAS System

The TTEST Procedure

Statistics

Variable	Class	N	Lower CL Mean	Mean	Upper CL Mean	Lower CL Std Dev	Std Dev
FRUST	0	117	11.518	12.282	13.046	3.696	4.1706
FRUST	1	39	11.449	12.872	14.295	3.5878	4.3901
FRUST	Diff (1-2)		-2.133	-0.59	0.9538	3.802	4.2258
FRUST	0	117	9.5107	10.274	11.036	3.692	4.166
FRUST	1	39	9.4487	10.872	12.295	3.5878	4.3901
FRUST	Diff (1-2)		-2.141	-0.598	0.944	3.7989	4.2224
SATIS	0	117	14.492	15.043	15.594	2.6673	3.0097
SATIS	1	39	12.469	13.667	14.864	3.0193	3.6945
SATIS	Diff (1-2)		0.21	1.3761	2.5421	2.8722	3.1924
INTENT	0	117	2.485	2.7179	2.9509	1.1273	1.272
INTENT	1	38	2.8571	3.3421	3.8271	1.2029	1.4755
INTENT	Diff (1-2)		-1.113	-0.624	-0.136	1.1909	1.3241
AGE	0	114	39.951	41.93	43.908	9.4346	10.662
AGE	1	39	33.384	36.795	40.206	8.6004	10.524
AGE	Diff (1-2)		1.2398	5.135	9.030	9.551	10.627

Statistics

Variable	Class		Upper CL Std Dev	Std Err	Minimum	Maximum
FRUST		0	4.7861	0.3856	5	20
FRUST		1	5.6578	0.703	5	20
FRUST	Diff (1-2)		4.7569	0.7814		
FRUST		0	4.7808	0.3851	3	18
FRUST		1	5.6578	0.703	3	18
FRUST	Diff (1-2)		4.753	0.7807		
SATIS		0	3.4539	0.2783	6	18
SATIS		1	4.7614	0.5916	3	18
SATIS	Diff (1-2)		3.5936	0.5903		
INTENT		0	1.4597	0.1176	1	6
INTENT		1	1.9089	0.2394	1	6
INTENT	Diff (1-2)		1.4911	0.2472		
AGE		0	12.259	0.9986	24	70
AGE		1	13.563	1.6851	23	62
AGE	Diff (1-2)		11.978	1.9714		

(continued)

```
(continued)

                               T-Tests

Variable   Method          Variances    DF    t Value    Pr > |t|

FRUST      Pooled          Equal        154    -0.75      0.4515
FRUST      Satterthwaite   Unequal      62.5   -0.74      0.4648
FRUST      Pooled          Equal        154    -0.77      0.4447
FRUST      Satterthwaite   Unequal      62.4   -0.75      0.4582
SATIS      Pooled          Equal        154     2.33      0.0210
SATIS      Satterthwaite   Unequal      55.8    2.10      0.0398
INTENT     Pooled          Equal        153    -2.52      0.0126
INTENT     Satterthwaite   Unequal      56     -2.34      0.0229
AGE        Pooled          Equal        151     2.60      0.0101
AGE        Satterthwaite   Unequal      66.6    2.62      0.0108


                        The TTEST Procedure

                      Equality of Variances

Variable     Method         Num DF   Den DF   F Value   Pr > F

FRUST        Folded F         38      116      1.11     0.6639
FRUST        Folded F         38      116      1.11     0.6577
SATIS        Folded F         38      116      1.51     0.1009
INTENT       Folded F         37      116      1.35     0.2377
AGE          Folded F        113       38      1.03     0.9570
```

ment. The 4th and 5th statements convert the continuous variable TENURE to two categories that represent above or below the median, which was 6 years. The remainder of the program contains PROCs to conduct multiple regression, one-way ANOVA, factorial ANOVA, and factor analysis.

Multiple Regression

Lines 6 and 7 in Program 9.7 conduct multiple regression. Line 6 tells SAS to run the REG procedure, which is one of several procedures that can be used for multiple regression. Line 7 is the MODEL statement, which allows you to define which variables are the criteria (dependent) and which are the predictors (independent). In this example, the criterion is intention of quitting (INTENT), and the predictors are SATIS, FRUST, AGE, and TENURE. After the variables are listed, there is a "/" which is followed by options. In this case, "STB" was added to indicate that standardized regression weights should be

Program 9.7
Program to Compute Some Complex Statistics

```
DATA COMPSTAT;
SET SASUSER.SURVEY;
TENURE = ROUND(TENURE/12);
IF TENURE < 7 THEN TENCAT = 1;
IF TENURE > 6 THEN TENCAT = 2;
PROC REG;
    MODEL INTENT = SATIS FRUST AGE TEN-
URE/STB;
PROC ANOVA;
   CLASS INTENT;
   MODEL SATIS = INTENT;
   MEANS INTENT/DUNCAN;
PROC GLM;
   CLASS QUIT TENCAT;
  MODEL FRUST = QUIT TENCAT QUIT*TENCAT;
   MEANS QUIT TENCAT QUIT*TENCAT;
PROC FACTOR PRIORS = S SCREE ROTATE =
VARIMAX;
    VAR ITEM1-ITEM6;
RUN;
```

output. Without this statement, only the unstandardized weights will be computed.

Output 9.7a shows the resulting output. At the top is an ANOVA source table that shows the results of an overall significance test relating the predictors to the criterion. In this case, the F was above 53, which was significant beyond the .0001 level. Below the source table, the R^2 and adjusted (for ratio of number of subjects to number of predictor variables) R^2 are shown. Further down are the results for the regression coefficients for each predictor and the intercept (or constant). The unstandardized coefficient is called the parameter estimate. The standard error, t test for significant difference from zero, and standardized estimate are shown. Job satisfaction, frustration, and age were all significant predictors, but tenure was not.

Output 9.7a

The SAS System

The REG Procedure
Model: MODEL1
Dependent Variable: INTENT

Analysis of Variance

Source	DF	Sum of Squares	Mean Square	F Value	Pr > F
Model	4	155.09799	38.77450	53.21	<.0001
Error	146	106.39870	0.72876		
Corrected Total	150	261.49669			

Root MSE	0.85367	R-Square	0.5931
Dependent Mean	2.84768	Adj R-Sq	0.5820
Coeff Var	29.97783		

Parameter Estimates

Variable	DF	Parameter Estimate	Standard Error	t Value	Pr > |t|	Standardized Estimate
Intercept	1	6.38116	0.56630	11.27	<.0001	0
SATIS	1	-0.22532	0.02550	-8.84	<.0001	-0.54767
FRUST	1	0.08169	0.01941	4.21	<.0001	0.26121
AGE	1	-0.02709	0.00669	-4.05	<.0001	-0.22150
TENURE	1	0.00716	0.01477	0.49	0.6284	0.02657

One-Way ANOVA

Simple one-way ANOVA and more complex factorial ANOVA can be conducted with PROC ANOVA as long as cell sample sizes are equal. In this example of a one-way ANOVA, the independent variable was INTENT with six levels, and the dependent variable was job satisfaction. To conduct an ANOVA, the CLASS statement lists the independent variable. The MODEL statement, similar to PROC REG, contains the dependent variable to the left of the equal sign and the independent variable(s) to the right. The MEANS statement indicates that we wish to have output the cell means for all levels of INTENT. To the right of the variable name is a slash followed by options. In this case, the keyword DUNCAN says to compute Duncan tests for the significance of each cell mean from the others.

Output 9.7b shows the resulting output. At the top, the output shows the independent variable and indicates how many levels it has. Five lines down is the source table that shows the significance test for the ANOVA. In this example, it is significant with an F of 30.79. There are two source tables. The upper one gives results for all independent variables combined, whereas the lower source table shows results for each independent variable and interaction separately. With only one independent variable, the results are the same in both places. At the bottom of the output are the cell means and results of the Duncan tests. In this case, the independent variable was a continuous variable, ranging from 1 to 6. As can be seen, the means on job satisfaction decreased linearly from the lowest to the highest value of intention to quit. The Duncans, however, show that the means for the first two INTENT groups (coded 1 and 2) were not significantly different from one another because the Duncan Grouping letters were both the same (A). The other groups had different letters, from B to E, meaning they were significantly different from one another.

Factorial ANOVA

Factorial ANOVA can be conducted with PROC ANOVA or with PROC GLM. The former PROC is simpler and can be used in many instances; however, it cannot be used when cell sizes are unequal in a factorial design. It can be with a one-way design. PROC GLM is a complex PROC that can be used to conduct ANOVA, multivariate ANOVA, analysis of covariance (ANCOVA), multivariate ANCOVA, and multiple regression. In this example, it was used to conduct a 2 × 2 factorial ANOVA with unequal sample sizes in the cells. The format for the commands for PROC GLM is similar to that for PROC ANOVA. The independent variables are listed on the CLASS statement. The MODEL statement lists the dependent variable to the left of the equal sign and the independent variables plus interactions to the right. The interactions are indicated with an asterisk ("*") between variables, as in

```
QUIT*TENCAT
```

You must list all effects you wish tested, as the program can run ANOVA with some effects omitted, such as higher order interactions. The MEANS statement

Output 9.7b

The SAS System

Analysis of Variance Procedure
Class Level Information

Class	Levels	Values
INTENT	6	1 2 3 4 5 6

Number of observations in data set = 156

NOTE: Due to missing values, only 155 observations can be used in this analysis.

Analysis of Variance Procedure

Dependent Variable: SATIS

Source	DF	Sum of Squares	Mean Square	F Value	Pr > F
Model	5	802.7849665	160.5569933	30.79	0.0001
Error	149	776.8924528	5.2140433		
Corrected Total	154	1579.6774194			

	R-Square	C.V.	Root MSE	SATIS Mean
	0.508196	15.48934	2.283428	14.74194

Source	DF	Anova SS	Mean Square	F Value	Pr > F
INTENT	5	802.7849665	160.5569933	30.79	0.0001

Analysis of Variance Procedure

Duncan's Multiple Range Test for variable: SATIS

NOTE: This test controls the type I comparisonwise error rate, not the experimentwise error rate

Alpha= 0.05 df= 149 MSE= 5.214043
WARNING: Cell sizes are not equal.
Harmonic Mean of cell sizes= 17.70943

Number of Means	2	3	4	5	6
Critical Range	1.516	1.596	1.649	1.688	1.718

Means with the same letter are not significantly different.

Duncan Grouping	Mean	N	INTENT
A	17.0833	24	1
A			
A	16.4000	40	2
B	14.8491	53	3
C	13.0000	17	4
D	11.3333	12	5
E	8.3333	9	6

indicates which level of means should be output. The individual variable names, such as QUIT, say to compute main effect means (i.e., the means for all subjects at each level of the variable QUIT). The interaction indicator says to compute means for the individual cells that make up the interaction. In this case, with two independent variables, it will produce cell means for each of the four cells.

The output is similar to that for PROC ANOVA in first showing the overall results for all independent variables followed by results for each main effect and interaction, and then providing means at the bottom. Output 9.7c shows that the overall ANOVA was significant with an F of 3.13. The R-Square gives an indication of the overall magnitude of effect, or how much of the variance in the dependent variable was explained by the independent variables, which in this case was .058233. The next section of the output shows results for each effect, but two different analyses are shown. The lower one, or Type III results, should be interpreted. It is adjusted appropriately for the unequal sample size in the design. In this case, only the interaction was significant. An inspection of the individual cell means shows why. Note that for QUIT, a value of 0 means the person didn't turn over (quit), and a value of 1 means that he or she did. Furthermore, a level of 1 for TENCAT means the person worked for the organization for less than 6 years, and a value of 2 means more than 6 years. Frustration was highest for (a) individuals who were fairly new hires and didn't quit and for (b) individuals who were long-term employees but did quit. In other words, high frustration was associated with quitting for new employees, but low frustration was associated with quitting for long-term employees. This perhaps reflects the fact that reasons for turnover differ between long- and short-term employees.

Factor Analysis

Factor analysis can be conducted with PROC FACTOR, as shown in Program 9.7. This PROC is quite flexible in conducting a number of different types of factor analysis, with a number of different options. For this example, the six items for the two scales (job satisfaction and organizational frustration) were analyzed. This was accomplished by listing the items by name (ITEM1-ITEM6) on the VAR statement that follows PROC FACTOR. Because the items were from different scales, we would hope they will produce two factors, with the items for each scale defining each factor. The PROC FACTOR statement contains options that tell SAS which type of analysis to conduct. PRIORS = S says to use the common factor model with the squared multiple correlations of each

Output 9.7c

The SAS System

The GLM Procedure

Class Level Information

Class	Levels	Values
QUIT	2	0 1
TENCAT	2	1 2

Number of observations in data set = 156

General Linear Models Procedure

Dependent Variable: FRUST

Source	DF	Sum of Squares	Mean Square	F Value	Pr > F
Model	3	160.495718	53.498573	3.13	0.0274
Error	152	2595.581205	17.076192		
Corrected Total	155	2756.076923			

R-Square	Coeff Var	Root MSE	FRUST Mean
0.058233	39.64602	4.132335	10.42308

Source	DF	Type I SS	Mean Square	F Value	Pr > F
QUIT	1	10.47008547	10.47008547	0.61	0.4348
TENCAT	1	67.74597281	67.74597281	3.97	0.0482
QUIT*TENCAT	1	82.27965989	82.27965989	4.82	0.0297

(continued)

(continued)

Source	DF	Type III SS	Mean Square	F Value	Pr > F
QUIT	1	0.01605734	0.01605734	0.00	0.9756
TENCAT	1	3.22224469	3.22224469	0.19	0.6646
QUIT*TENCAT	1	82.27965989	82.27965989	4.82	0.0297

The GLM Procedure

Level of QUIT	N	————FRUST———— Mean	Std Dev
0	117	10.2735043	4.16600348
1	39	10.8717949	4.39005747

Level of TENCAT	N	————FRUST———— Mean	Std Dev
1	100	9.9500000	4.16909020
2	56	11.2678571	4.20601764

Level of QUIT	Level of TENCAT	N	————FRUST———— Mean	Std Dev
0	1	72	9.4305556	3.96756707
0	2	45	11.6222222	4.16308937
1	1	28	11.2857143	4.44603146
1	2	11	9.8181818	4.26188179

variable with all others as estimates of communalities. It is possible to choose other models with a MODEL statement (not shown here), and there are other options for communality estimates. SCREE says to output the scree plot to aid in determining number of factors to rotate. ROTATE = VARIMAX allows for choice of varimax orthogonal rotation. Other types of rotation are also available. The next statement lists the variables to analyze.

Output 9.7d shows the results. Communality estimates for each of the six items are shown first. Below this are the eigenvalues for each item. Next is the scree plot. An inspection of the eigenvalues shows that two are positive, and the remaining four are negative and quite close to zero. This, in combination with the scree plot, suggests that two factors should be rotated. Below the scree plot are the factor loadings, first before and then after rotation. The rotated factor pattern shows that the first three items from the frustration scale loaded positively on factor 2, with large loadings, and negatively with quite small loadings on factor 1. The results for items 4 to 6 from the job satisfaction scale are the opposite. This provides evidence for two clear-cut factors, each containing items from only one of the two scales.

COMMON ERRORS

The most important thing to do with any data set before analysis is to check for errors. Once all data are entered, you should run checks for out of range values and impossible combinations, as shown in Chapter 4 (see Program 4.1). Another approach is to put in commands to set equal to "missing" any variable value that is not within possible range (e.g., if a variable can range from 1 to 4, any value less than 1 or greater than 4 is set to missing). Of course, it is better to investigate the cause of the discrepant value and fix it, but this is not always possible.

As can be seen in the examples here, using PROCs can be very easy, but they are also easy to use incorrectly. As long as the syntax is correct, you will get output that might look correct but actually be wrong. Before using any PROC, you should be well versed in the statistic you are trying to use. Furthermore, you should always begin with simple statistics and build up to more complex ones, and then examine all the results carefully to be sure they make sense. The better you understand the statistics, the more able you will be to detect when things don't make sense. More often than not, when they don't make sense, an error was made.

RESOURCES FOR INFORMATION ABOUT USING PROCS

There are many resources available for help with PROCs. In the Windows version of SAS, the help provides online documentation that shows the syntax for PROCs and all the available options. More extensive documentation can

Output 9.7d

The SAS System

Initial Factor Method: Principal Factors

Prior Communality Estimates: SMC

ITEM1	ITEM2	ITEM3	ITEM4	ITEM5	ITEM6
0.569608	0.427334	0.592135	0.679111	0.743564	0.536202

Eigenvalues of the Reduced Correlation Matrix:
Total = 3.54795461 Average = 0.59132577

	1	2	3
Eigenvalue	3.1117	0.8120	-0.0261
Difference	2.2998	0.8381	0.0307
Proportion	0.8770	0.2289	-0.0074
Cumulative	0.8770	1.1059	1.0985

	4	5	6
Eigenvalue	-0.0568	-0.1248	-0.1680
Difference	0.0680	0.0432	
Proportion	-0.0160	-0.0352	-0.0473
Cumulative	1.0825	1.0473	1.0000

2 factors will be retained by the PROPORTION criterion.

Initial Factor Method: Principal Factors

Scree Plot of Eigenvalues

```
         '
3.5    _
         '
         '
         '
                       1
3.0    _
         '
         '
         '
2.5    _
         '
         '
         '
E 2.0  _
i        '
g        '
e        '
n        '
v 1.5  _
a        '
l        '
u        '
e        '
s 1.0  _
         '
                      2
         '
         '
         '
```

(continued)

(continued)

```
 0.5  _
           ,
           ,
           ,
 0.0  _    '
           ,              3
           ,                      4       5
           ,                                    6
           ,
-0.5  _    '
      Sffffffff^ffffffff^ffffffff^ffffffff^ffffffff^ffffffff^ffffffff^ffffffff^ffffffff
         0         1        2        3        4        5        6
```

Number

Initial Factor Method: Principal Factors

Factor Pattern

	FACTOR1	FACTOR2
ITEM1	-0.68367	0.43408
ITEM2	-0.59094	0.38032
ITEM3	-0.72914	0.35104
ITEM4	0.75022	0.41204
ITEM5	0.82482	0.35894
ITEM6	0.72133	0.23885

Variance explained by each factor

FACTOR1	FACTOR2
3.111722	0.811957

Final Communality Estimates: Total = 3.923679

ITEM1	ITEM2	ITEM3	ITEM4	ITEM5	ITEM6
0.655826	0.493852	0.654874	0.732604	0.809160	0.577362

Rotation Method: Varimax

Orthogonal Transformation Matrix

	1	2
1	0.74590	-0.66606
2	0.66606	0.74590

Rotated Factor Pattern

	FACTOR1	FACTOR2
ITEM1	-0.22082	0.77914
ITEM2	-0.18747	0.67728
ITEM3	-0.31006	0.74749
ITEM4	0.83403	-0.19235
ITEM5	0.85431	-0.28164
ITEM6	0.69713	-0.30229

Variance explained by each factor

FACTOR1	FACTOR2
2.091475	1.832203

(continued)

```
(continued)

Final Communality Estimates: Total = 3.923679

          ITEM1      ITEM2      ITEM3      ITEM4      ITEM5    ITEM6
        0.655826   0.493852   0.654874   0.732604   0.809160 0.577362
```

be found in the various procedures manuals for the Release 6.x family and 8.x family. With Release 8.x, SAS has been moving toward providing documentation electronically, and the contents of the manuals are available on CD-ROM as well as paper. Books also are available that explain how to conduct various statistical analyses with SAS. Some were published by the SAS Institute, and some were not. Finally, the SAS Institute Web site (http://www.sas.com) contains a great deal of information about how to use the software. Below are the references to the SAS Institute *PROC* manuals. A more extensive list of books is in Appendix D.

SAS Procedures Guide, Version 6 (3rd ed.), 1990.
SAS Procedures Guide, Version 8, 1999.
SAS/STAT® User's Guide, Version 6 (4th ed., Vols. 1 and 2), 1990.
SAS/STAT User's Guide, Version 8, 1999.

The SAS guides cover the basic PROCs, whereas the SAS/STAT guides cover the more advanced procedures. For the most part, Release 8.x offers enhancements over release 6.x and is backwardly compatible, so manuals written for 6.x should work for 8.x. Appendix C of this book provides a list of the PROCs most commonly used, at least in the social sciences.

NOTE

1. The data set used for the examples in this chapter was taken from a study of university clerical workers (Spector, 1991; Spector, Dwyer, & Jex, 1988). For the purposes of these examples, a limited subset of data from the study was taken; it can be found on my Web site (http://chuma. cas.usf.edu/~spector).

Chapter 10

Final Advice on Becoming a SAS® Programmer

If you have read this book carefully, and entered, run, and experimented with the examples, you should have a fairly good sense of the SAS language. You should be able to write your own programs and may be ready to tackle fairly complex problems. As with any skill, like playing golf or riding a bicycle, the learning comes primarily from practice. The more you program, the better you will get and the easier you will find it becomes.

This chapter will discuss three issues that will enable you to write better and more successful programs. First, you need to carefully debug and test your programs. A program that runs without a SAS error is not necessarily running correctly. Second, there are many different ways to approach a particular programming problem. You should consider the advantages and disadvantages of particular features and approaches that you might use. Finally, prior planning can make programming go more smoothly. Even experienced programmers have a difficult time sitting down "cold" in front of the computer and writing a program with no prior planning.

DEBUGGING AND TESTING
A PROGRAM REVISITED

The issue of debugging a program has been discussed throughout this book. It is one aspect of programming that can be very discouraging for the novice programmer. It seems that no matter how carefully you plan, write, and proof-read your programs, they never seem to run without errors initially. Errors are important learning tools, particularly for the new programmer. Each program is like an examination: You test your understanding of the SAS language with the problem you are programming. Errors can indicate that your understanding of some concept or statement was incorrect. The process of figuring out why the error occurred and how to fix it is the process of learning to program. To some extent, this requires a trial-and-error process of entering statements to see what they do and experimenting until you get your program to do what you want it to do.

Some strategies for debugging have already been discussed. To summarize, you must always check the SAS Log to uncover errors. The error messages and warnings will indicate if there have been syntax errors. Furthermore, you should look carefully at the information provided about the number of cases and variables for each data file. This can be an important clue that something isn't working properly. Once the SAS Log errors have been fixed, you must test the program to be sure it works properly. Test problems that already have been worked out should be run and checked against an independently computed answer. It can also be helpful to use PUT statements to output intermediate calculations to test that they are working properly. Often this can be done easily by entering a small problem that is worked out by hand. Logical errors are extremely easy to make, so you can't be too thorough in testing your program.

ALTERNATE APPROACHES

Many approaches can be taken for most programming tasks. Don't be too concerned at first that you have found the "best" or "correct" way to program a problem. If your program does what you need it to do, it is correct. As you gain experience with SAS programming, you will develop a programming style. There may be certain approaches that you will prefer over others, and there may be certain ways that you approach problems. Even with fairly simple programming tasks, different programmers will write very different programs that all yield the intended results. Most of the examples in this book could have been done in many other ways. A useful exercise would be to try to rewrite an example program from the book using your own approach and style.

Some features of the SAS language have definite advantages over others. You have seen how loops and arrays can make programs efficient when repetitive operations are performed, as in scoring a psychological test. For some situations, the approach you use is merely an issue of personal preference. For example, to output the square of the numbers 1 to 3, you could use a loop:

```
DO I = 1, 4, 9;
PUT I;
END;
```

or you could use three PUT statements:

```
PUT 1;
PUT 4;
PUT 9;
```

Both approaches use the same number of statements. There is little reason to prefer one over the other.

There is one style of programming that you should attempt to avoid, and that involves the extensive use of the GOTO statement. Chapter 5 discussed how too many GOTOs can lead to spaghetti code—a program that skips around so much from place to place that it becomes very difficult to trace and debug. Although a poorly organized program may still get the job done, it is best to employ good organization.

Two rules for the use of GOTOs will help avoid poorly organized programs. First, try to write your programs so that branching returns you from where you branched. This occurs automatically when you use LINK. This is not always possible, but programs organized such that a main section sends execution to a subsection and back are easier to trace. Figure 5.1 illustrates a program that is organized in this way. The alternative, where line 10 sends you to line 40, which sends you to line 20, which sends you to line 15, which sends you to line 50, which sends you to line 10, becomes a convoluted trail of logic that is very difficult to follow.

Second, avoid using a GOTO statement within a loop. Many times, you can use a DO WHILE or DO UNTIL instead to end the loop when a certain value is reached. It makes program tracing easier when you don't have to be concerned with branching within a loop. Thus, instead of

```
DO I = 1 to 10;
   Y = X/I;
   IF Y = 4 THEN GOTO LABA;
   IF Y = 8 THEN GOTO LABB;
END;
```

you can use

```
I = 0;
DO UNTIL (Y = 4 or Y = 8 or I = 10);
   I = I + 1;
   Y = X/I;
END;
IF Y = 4 THEN LINK A;
IF Y = 8 THEN LINK B;
```

These rules make tracing easier, but they can't always be followed, nor should they be rigidly adhered to. Minimizing the extent to which GOTOs jump around a program, however, will make for easier debugging, testing, and program modification.

ADVANCE PLANNING

As discussed earlier, it is easier to write a program if you take time to plan the program in advance. The larger and more complex the program, the more important it is to do adequate preplanning, which can occur in stages. First, you should consider the purpose of the program and design the contents and appearance of the output. Next, you need to specify the major tasks that need to be done in their appropriate order. From this, you can create a flowchart of the major components of the program. The more detailed the flowchart, the easier it will be to write the program. Examples of flowcharts can be found in several places in this book. If you need to, you can write the program in pseudocode, as described in Chapter 1. Finally, you can write out the SAS statements for your program.

Large programs might be best approached in stages, in which you plan each stage separately. In fact, it might be best to plan, write, and debug each stage before going on to the next. Sometimes an error in logic at one stage can have a significant effect on the approach taken in later stages. This may not become apparent until you debug.

Remember that in programming, correct order is everything. Computers are relentless, carrying out your instructions step by step by step until the end of the program is reached. The computer knows only what you have told it previously, as it carries out each instruction. As each instruction is encountered, ask yourself if you have told the computer everything it needs to know in order to complete your task correctly. Once you have planned out the orderly flow of instructions, you can fill in the actual SAS statements.

HOW TO BECOME A GOOD PROGRAMMER

Perhaps the two biggest impediments to learning how to program are lack of confidence and impatience. Lack of confidence is expressed as a feeling that programming is so difficult that only computer experts can program. By now, you should have an appreciation that programming is logical and straightforward, and not impossibly difficult. As with any skill, it seems much harder to learn until you have mastered it. The way to build up your confidence is with experience and practice. Begin with small programs and slowly build your skill to take on larger and larger programming tasks. As your skill grows, self-confidence should grow with it.

The second problem is that people often become impatient with the prospect of having to take the time to learn programming. A person may have a need for programming, but he or she may not like computers or really be interested in programming. Many people feel that computers should be so easy to use that very little learning is necessary. Perhaps they should be, but unfortunately they are not.

Often, the motivation to learn programming arises from a real problem that a person needs to solve. For example, a graduate student may need programming to complete a master's thesis or doctoral dissertation. A researcher may need to write a program to analyze data for a research paper. Under the press of time to complete a project, it is common to become impatient with having to learn a new skill. Unfortunately, there are no shortcuts to learning. It takes time and practice to become proficient with the SAS language—or any computer language. If you have no programming experience at all, plan on spending some time to learn the skill, and don't become discouraged if you don't progress as quickly as you would like.

The SAS language is a powerful tool, not only for researchers in the social sciences but in any area where statistical data need to be analyzed. It also is of value to nonresearchers who use statistical data, for example, managers, human resource professionals, and information specialists. Whereas the examples used in this book were focused toward research applications, the programming principles can be applied to other types of problems. SAS programming can be an important skill for individuals who need to manipulate and analyze statistical information. The investment of some time and effort can return a useful and highly marketable skill.

Appendix A

Definitions of Useful Programming Terms

Accumulator: Variable that contains the result of computations across either other variables or other cases

Argument: Number or variable to be evaluated by a function

Arithmetic operator: Symbol that indicates an operation, such as a plus ("+") or minus ("−") sign

Array: Single variable name that can represent two or more variables distinguished by superscript number (e.g., X(4)

Branching: Command that causes some cases to be treated differently from others depending upon the value of one or more variables.

Case: The sampling unit, such as a subject, upon which observations are taken. SAS organizes data by cases

Concatenation: Vertical combination of separate data sets that have the same variables but different cases

Counter: A variable that keeps track of the number of cases or the times a certain operation has been done

Delimiter: A character that is used in a data set to separate variables (e.g., a blank space or a comma)

Expression: A statement that defines a variable as a function of a number or other variable(s)

Flag: A variable that keeps track of a condition (e.g., keeps track of even and odd cases)

Function: A built-in expression to accomplish an operation (e.g., taking a square root)

Index variable: With a Do loop, the variable that specifies the number of iterations of the loop; with arrays, it specifies the array element

Initialization: Providing a starting value, usually zero, for an accumulator, counter, or other variable

Iterate: To repeat an operation, as in a Do loop

Listwise deletion: With statistics involving more than two variables, analyzing only cases that have nonmissing data for all variables (*see also* pairwise deletion)

Logical error: A program that has all statements in proper form but does not do what was intended

Merging: Horizontal combination of files in which each has the same cases but different variables

Nested Do loops: Loops that are contained within one another so that the inner loop repeats its complete series of iterations once for each iteration of the outer loop. Note that this can be disrupted with a statement within the loops

Pairwise deletion: Keeping the maximum number of cases for each statistic computed, even if some cases have missing values for additional variables. For example, with PROC CORR, pairwise deletion would compute correlations for each pair of variables, deleting only cases missing one of those two variables, even if other variables are missing for a case, possibly resulting in different sample sizes for each individual correlation computed (*see also* listwise deletion)

Pointer location: The column position within a data line from which the program will read data, starting with the pointer in the first column and moving from left to right unless redirected by the INPUT statement

Seed: The number used by a random number generator as a starting value. The time on the computer's clock is commonly used

Syntax error: An error caused by a statement that is either internally inconsistent or in a form that the computer does not recognize, similar to either a grammar or spelling error in English

Appendix B

Summary of SAS Language Statements

Command	Example	Purpose
ARRAY	**Array** item(10) x1-x10;	Defines an array of specified size with specified variables as elements
CARDS	**cards**;	Indicates that input data will follow
DATA	**data** group1;	Begins a data step and assigns a name
DELETE	if n > 11 then **delete**	Eliminates cases from the data set
DO index =	**do** i = 1 to 10;	Begins a Do loop that will execute the number of times specified by the index
DO UNTIL	**do until** count = 50;	Begins a loop that will continue until the specified condition is met
DO WHILE	**do while** count < 50;	Begins a loop that will continue until specified condition no longer occurs
DROP	**drop** gender;	Eliminates variables from the data set
ELSE	if gender = 1 then n = n + 1; **else** return;	Specifies what to do with every case that isn't covered by preceding IF statement(s)
END	do i = 1 to 10; count = count + 1; **end**;	Signals the end of a Do loop

FILE	**file** "c:/data/scored.dat";	Indicates name of file for outputting
GOTO	**goto** a:	Tells SAS to skip to the part of the program marked with the specified label
IF	**if** age > 18;	Says to keep case if it meets specified condition
IF . . . THEN	**if** party = "d" then do;	Indicates condition under which a statement or statements should be executed
INFILE	**Infile**"c:/data/ cohort1.dat";	Indicates name of file for inputting
INPUT	**input** x 1. y 4.;	Specifies names of variables to be input and their formats
KEEP	keep name income;	Lists names of variables to be kept in the data set
LINK	link a:	Tells SAS to skip to the part of the program marked with the specified label, execute commands until reaching a RETURN, and then skip to the statement following LINK
MERGE	**merge** first second; by id;	Used to horizontally combine files containing the same cases
PUT	**put** "identification = " id 4. "Status = " stat 2.;	Lists variables to be output in specified format as well as messages to be output
RETAIN	**retain** accum 0;	Overrides automatic resetting with each new case for value of specified variable, and gives its starting value
RETURN	**return**;	When used with LINK, signals end of statement block; when used without LINK, says to enter the next case
STOP	**stop**;	Causes SAS program to cease immediately

Appendix C

Summary of Popular SAS PROCs

PROC	Statistical Procedure	Comments
ANOVA*	Analysis of variance	Balanced designs (equal sample size) only
CALIS	Structural equation modeling	Alternative to LISREL or EQS
CANCOR	Canonical correlation	
CATMOD	Log linear and logistic procedures	General program for many different analyses based on contingency tables
CLUSTER	Cluster analysis	Can do 11 different types of cluster analysis
CONTENTS	Show contents of SAS data library	
CORR*	Correlation	Can also do item analysis
CORRESP	Correspondence analysis	
DISCRIM	Discriminant analysis	Can do both parametric and nonparametric approaches
FACTOR	Factor analysis	Does several models and different kinds of rotations
FASTCLUS	Cluster analysis	Disjoints clustering for large data sets

FREQ*	Frequency tables	Computes one-variable frequency tables and multivariable contingency tables; can do some inferential tests on contingency tables
GLM*	Analysis of variance and covariance, multiple regression, multivariate analysis of variance and covariance	A general linear models program; must be used for unbalanced (unequal sample size) ANOVA designs
LIFEREG	Survival analysis	Does parametric failure time analysis
LOGISTIC	Logistic regression	Does analysis for binary or ordinal criterion (dependent) variable
MDS	Multidimensional scaling	Does MDS using a variety of different models
MEANS	Descriptive statistics	For continuous variables
NLIN	Nonlinear regression	
NPAR1WAY	Analysis of variance on rank data	Limited to a one-way design
ORTHOREG	Multiple regression using the Gentleman-Givens method	Useful when data don't meet requirements for more standard regression procedures
PLOT*	Graph two variables	Provides scatterplot of two variables
PRINCOMP	Principal components analysis	
PRINT*	Lists values of all variables	
PROBIT	Logistic regression	Preferred over LOGISTIC for some applications
RANK	Computes ranks for cases on a variable	
REG*	Multiple regression	General regression procedure recommended for most problems
RSREG	Response surface analysis	
SCORE	Produce linear combinations	Applies weights from one matrix to scores in another; useful for computing factor scores
SORT*	Sort cases on one or more variables	Needed before using a BY option with MERGE or PROCs
STEPDISC	Stepwise discriminant analysis	Does backward, forward, and stepwise procedures

TTEST*	*t* test	Provides adjustment for unequal variances
UNIVARIATE	Descriptive statistics	Provides more statistics than MEANS
VARCLUS	Cluster analysis of correlation or covariance matrix	

*Example shown in this book.

SAS PROCs

Appendix D

Sources of Information About Using SAS PROCs for Statistical Analysis

Below is a list of some sources that might be useful for using PROCs. This is not an endorsement of these sources, as I've not seen many of them. A more extensive list can be found in the SAS Publications Catalog, which is available in electronic (www.sas.com/pubs) or printed form. Keep in mind that many of these sources were written for Release 6 of SAS, so there may be some differences between what's in the book and Release 8.

Applied Multivariate Statistics With SAS Software (2nd ed.). (1999). Ravindra Khattree & Dayanand N. Naik.

Applied Statistics and the SAS Programming Language (4th ed.). (1997). Ron Cody & Jeffrey K. Smith.

Categorical Data Analysis Using the SAS System. (1995). Maura E. Stokes, Charles S. Davis, & Gary G. Koch.

Common Statistical Methods for Clinical Research With SAS Examples. (1997). Glenn A. Walker.

Extending SAS Survival Analysis Techniques for Medical Research. (1997). Alan Cantor.

Forecasting Examples for Business and Economics Using the SAS System. (1996). David A. Dickey.

A Handbook of Statistical Analyses Using SAS. (1997). B. S. Everitt & G. Der.

Integrating Results Through Meta-Analytic Review Using SAS Software. (1999). M. C. Wang & Brad J. Bushman.

Introduction to Market Research Using the SAS System. (1994). SAS Institute.

Logistic Regression Examples Using the SAS System, Version 6. (1995). SAS Institute.

Logistic Regression Using the SAS System: Theory and Applications. (1999). Paul D. Allison.

Models for Discrete Data. (1999). Daniel Zelterman.

Multiple Comparisons and Multiple Tests Using the SAS System. (1999). Peter H. Westfall, Randall D. Tobias, Dror Rom, Russell D. Wolfinger, & Yosef Hochberg.

Multivariate Data Reduction and Discrimination With SAS Software. (2000). Ravindra Khatree & Dayanand N. Naik.

SAS System for Elementary Statistical Analysis (2nd ed.). (1997). Sandra D. Schlotzhauer & Ramon C. Littell.

SAS System for Linear Models (3rd ed.). (1991). Ramon C. Littell, Rudolf J. Freund, & Philip C. Spector.

SAS System for Mixed Models. (1996). Ramon C. Littell, George A. Milliken, Walter W. Stroup, & Russell D. Wolfinger.

SAS System for Regression (3rd ed.). (2000). Rudolf J. Freund & Ramon C. Littell.

The SAS Workbook. (1996). Ron Cody.

Statistical Quality Control Using the SAS System. (1996). Dennis W. King.

A Step-by-Step Approach to Using the SAS System for Factor Analysis and Structural Equation Modeling. (1994). Larry Hatcher.

A Step-by-Step Approach to Using the SAS System for Univariate and Multivariate Statistics. (1994). Larry Hatcher & Edward J. Stepanski.

Survival Analysis Using the SAS System: A Practical Guide. (1995). Paul D. Allison.

Univariate and Multivariate General Linear Models: Theory and Applications Using SAS Software. (1997). Neil H. Timm & Tammy A. Mieczkowski.

INFORMATION SOURCES

Appendix E

Corrections to the Debugging Exercises

Exercise 1.1

1. The variable "E" is missing from the INPUT statement in the second line of the program.

Exercise 1.2

1. There shouldn't be a semicolon ";" at the end of the data in the 8th line.

Exercise 2.1

1. Semicolon missing from input statement.
2. Statement beginning with "total =" must come before the datalines command.

Exercise 2.2

1. Dollar sign "$" is missing from INPUT statement after "state" to indicate character variable.
2. First two PUT statements should have at the beginning "If _n_ = 1 then" to have it print these headers only once.
3. Insert "@25" after "State" on second PUT statement.

Exercise 3.1

1. In the third line, the mean function refers to "x11" and "x12," which are variables that have not been defined.

2. In the 4th line, the value of "x6" is negative and is not a valid argument to the square root function.

3. In the 5th line, there is a closed parenthesis missing before the "+x2".

Exercise 3.2

1. There are three errors here that partially counteract one another. Line 3 is missing a semicolon, which means it and the next statement are considered one statement. Line 3 is missing a right parenthesis and line 4 is missing a left parenthesis. Thus, the parentheses will balance across the two statements, and as written the program will not produce an error message about parentheses. Once the semicolon is fixed, error messages will suggest that parentheses are unbalanced.

Exercise 4.1

This program has no syntax errors—only logical ones. When you first run it, there will be no error messages, so you will have to find the three errors without these hints.

1. The counter variable "n" is missing from the RETAIN statement in line 5.
2. The logical statement in line 6 needs an "or" rather than "and."
3. In line 8, to the right of the equal sign, add "sumheight +".

Exercise 4.2

This program is supposed to compute separate means for males (coded m) and females (coded f) on height in inches. Adding a PROC PRINT might help you trace the problems.

1. "Gender" is a character variable, but in the "if gender =" statements the parentheses are missing around the values, that is, "m" and "f." SAS interprets the "f" and "m" as variable names, and those variables are uninitialized.

2. In line 11, "sumheightf" is misspelled.

3. In the two statements that compute the means, the counters were reversed, so the female sum is divided by the male sample size, and vice versa.

Exercise 5.1

This program counts the number of people who are under 72 inches tall. It has two syntax errors and one logical error.

1. The comment in the first line is missing the leading asterisk.

2. Prior to the data, the DATALINES statement is "data" by mistake.

3. As written, the program executes the statements following the count label twice for each case under 72 inches and once for those 72 inches or more. A RETURN statement is needed before the "count" label to prevent execution of the counter statement when it isn't intended.

Exercise 5.2

This program is a modification of Exercise 4.2, using links to different portions of the program.

1. The DATA statement is missing the semicolon.

2. The male portion of the program is missing its RETURN statement.

3. The label statement called "means" should be ended by a colon, not a semicolon.

Exercise 6.1

1. The variable "n" should be initialized at 0, not 1.

2. On the DO WHILE statement, it should be "n =< 10" and not "n = 10."

Exercise 6.2

1. The same index variable is used for both loops. The inner one should be changed from "i" to "i" or some other variable name.

2. Four different means are computed, so the "sumx" variable should be reset each time. Move the statement that sets "sumx" to zero after the first DO statement.

Exercise 7.1

1. The DO statement sets values of "i" from 1 to 12, but there are only 10 elements of the "x" array. The maximum value for the index variable in this loop can be only 10.

2. Inside the Do loop, the "x" array is mentioned without an indication of the element number, as in "x(i)." The "i" must match the index variable on the DO statement.

Exercise 7.2

1. The index variables "i" and "i" on the two DO statements should be reversed. The inner loop should have "i" and the outer loop should have "i."

2. In order to have the program print the rows of the matrix across the page, insert an "@" at the end of the PUT statement that is inside the innermost loop.

Exercise 8.1

1. The input statements for "file1" and "file2" failed to indicate that the "party" and "voted" variables were character rather than numeric.

2. The purpose of this program was to concatenate, not merge. The SET statement should have been used rather than MERGE.

Exercise 8.2

1. The cases are not in the same order, so match merging does not work properly. A BY statement is needed to combine cases according to the ID variable.

2. When using a BY statement, each file must first be sorted—in this case, according to the ID variable.

REFERENCES

Cammann, C., Fichman, M., Jenkins, D., & Klesh, J. (1979). *The Michigan Organizational Assessment Questionnaire.* Unpublished manuscript, University of Michigan, Ann Arbor.

Namboodiri, K. (1984). *Matrix algebra: An introduction* (Sage University Papers series on Quantitative Applications in the Social Sciences, 07-038). Beverly Hills, CA: Sage.

Peters, L. H., & O'Connor, E. J. (1980). The behavioral and affective consequences of performance-related situational variables. *Organizational Behavior and Human Performance, 25,* 79-96.

SAS® Companion for Microsoft Windows Environment Version 8. (1999). Cary, NC: SAS Institute Inc.

SAS® Language: Reference, Version 6 (1st ed.). (1990). Cary, NC: SAS Institute Inc.

SAS Procedures Guide, Version 6 (3rd ed.). (1990). Cary, NC: SAS Institute Inc.

SAS Procedures Guide, Version 8. (1999). Cary, NC: SAS Institute Inc.

SAS® Language Reference: Dictionary Version 8 (Vols. 1 and 2). (1999). Cary, NC: SAS Institute Inc.

SAS/STAT® User's Guide, Version 6 (4th ed., Vols. 1 and 2). (1989). Cary, NC: SAS Institute Inc.

SAS/STAT® User's Guide, Version 8 (4th ed., Vols. 1-3). (1999). Cary, NC: SAS Institute Inc.

Spector, P. E. (1991). Confirmatory test of a turnover model utilizing multiple data sources. *Human Performance, 4,* 221-230.

Spector, P. E. (1992). *Summated rating scale construction: An introduction* (Sage University Paper series on Quantitative Applications in the Social Sciences, 07-082). Newbury Park, CA: Sage.

Spector, P. E., Dwyer, D. J., & Jex, S. M. (1988). Relations of job stressors to affective, health, and performance outcomes. *Journal of Applied Psychology, 73,* 11-19.

INDEX

Accumulator, 86
Arguments, in functions, 59
Arithmetic operators, 56-58
    priority, 57
ARRAY statement, 132
    array, multidimensional, 139-144
    array, one dimensional, 132-134
ASCII, 32, 158
Asterisk. *See* comment
Branching, 95

BY statement, 157-159

CARDS statement, 28, 32, 34
Character values, 38
Coin flip simulation, 117-118
Column locations, 35
Comment, 21-22
Computer languages, 2-3
Concatenation, 153-155
Conditional statement. *See* IF . . .
    THEN statement
Counter, 86

DATA= option, 44
Data file, 29-30, 32-33
Data set name, 4
DATA statement, 28-31
Data step, 4, 28

DATALINES statement, 22, 28, 32, 34
Debugging, 17-20, 52-53, 210
DELETE statement, 82
Delimiter, 38-39
DELIMITER option, 39
DO INDEX= statement, 112-113
Do loops, 111-121
DO UNTIL statement, 113-115
DO WHILE statement, 115-117
DROP statement, 67-68

EBCDIC, 158
ELSE statement, 81-82
END option, 83, 112
END statement, 84
End of file, detecting, 83-84
Endless loop, 108, 114, 116
Errors, 18-20, 53, 71-72, 91-92,
    107-108, 126-127, 141, 150-151,
    173, 203
EXCEL file, 12
Expressions, 56-58

F key functions, 9
File names, 33
FILE statement, 34, 52, 163
Flag, 99-103
Flowchart, 16-17, 89, 106, 108, 125
Formatting output, 143-144

Functions. *See* SAS functions

GO TO statement, 96

Help, 22-24
Holding the input line, 40-41

IF . . . statement, 83-84
IF . . . THEN statement, 49, 75-79,
    81-82
Index variable, 112-113
INFILE statement, 33
INPUT statement, 34-41
Inputting, 34-35
Interface, 6-12

Justification, 35

KEEP statement, 67-68

Label, 96-97
Label names, 96
LINK statement, 97
List input, 38-39
Log, 8, 10, 13, 14, 19-20
Logical operators, 75-79
    table of, 77
Logical statements, 75-81
Loop, endless. *See* Endless loop
LRECL option, 39

Matrices, 139-150
 Matrix operations, 144-147
    multiplication, 146-147
    transpose, 146
MERGE statement, 155-157
Merging, 154-157
Missing values, 37-39, 171-172
MISSOVER option, 37-38, 53
Monte Carlo study, 111, 117

_N_ variable, 49, 75-78
Nested loops, 118-121
Operators. *See* Arithmetic operators,
    Logical operators

Output format. *See* PUT statement
Output location, 42-43
Output statement, 41-42, 98, 162-163
Outputting, 41-51

Planning a program, 15-17, 212-213
Pointer location, 36
PROC, 4
PROC ANOVA, 197-199
PROC CORR, 179-181
PROC FACTOR, 200, 202-206
PROC FREQ, 181-189
PROC GLM, 198-202
PROC MEANS, 190-191
PROC PLOT, 190-192
PROC PRINT, 30, 44-45, 52
PROC REG, 195-197
PROC SORT, 158-159
PROC TTEST, 91, 192-195
Program editor, 7-8, 10-11
Program flow, 105-107
Pseudocode, 16-17
PUT statements, 43-44, 48-51, 52,
    163

Random number generator, 64-65
Report writing, 48-51
RETAIN statement, 85
RETURN statement, 97-98
Right justification, 35

SAS data library, 28, 32-34, 157,
    159-161
SAS functions, 59-68
    absolute value, 59-61
    combination, 63
    descriptive statistics, 61-63
    exponential, 63
    factorial, 63
    log, 63
    mod, 63
    permutation, 63
    probability distributions, 64-65
    random number generators, 64-65
    rounding functions, 65-66

square root, 59
table of functions, 60
trigonomic functions, 66-67
ZIP code, 59
SAS log, 8, 10, 13-14, 19-20, 39
SAS Manuals, 23, 206
SAS releases, 4-6
SAS Statements, 21-22
SAS versions, 4-6
Scatterplot, 190-192
Scoring tests, 134-139
SET statement, 154
Simulation, 117-118, 121-126
Sort orders, 158-159
Sorting files. *See* PROC SORT statement
Spaghetti code, 107-108, 211
SCP matrix, 145, 147-150

STOP statement, 98
Storage devices, 30, 32
Subscript out of range error, 141, 150
Sum of squares and cross products matrix. *See* SSCP matrix

t-test, 87-91, 192-195
simulation, 121-127
Turnover, 178-179

Variable formats, 41
Variable names, 35
Variable uninitialized error, 68

W.d Formats, 35-38
Windows, 5-6

ABOUT THE AUTHOR

Paul E. Spector is Professor and Director of the Industrial/Organizational Psychology Program at the University of South Florida. His interests include both content (counterproductive work behavior, employee well-being, job satisfaction, job stress, and personality) and methodology. He has published in many of the leading journals of the field, including *Academy of Management Journal*, *Journal of Applied Psychology*, *Journal of Management*, and *Psychological Bulletin*. He is an associate editor for *Journal of Occupational and Organizational Psychology* and the point/counterpoint editor for *Journal of Organizational Behavior*. He has written two books in the Sage Quantitative Methods in the Social Science series and one on job satisfaction for the Sage Advanced Topics in Organizational Behavior series. He also has written an industrial/organizational psychology textbook.